Jerry J. Bigner, PhD
Joseph L. Wetchler, PhD
Editors

Relationship Therapy with Same-Sex Couples

Relationship Therapy with Same-Sex Couples has been co-published simultaneously as *Journal of Couple & Relationship Therapy*, Volume 3, Numbers 2/3 2004.

Pre-publication
REVIEWS,
COMMENTARIES,
EVALUATIONS . . .

The Haworth Press, Inc.

Relationship Therapy with Same-Sex Couples

Relationship Therapy with Same-Sex Couples has been co-published simultaneously as *Journal of Couple & Relationship Therapy*, Volume 3, Numbers 2/3 2004.

The *Journal of Couple & Relationship Therapy* Monographic "Separates" (formerly the *Journal of Couples Therapy* series)*

Below is a list of "separates," which in serials librarianship means a special issue simultaneously published as a special journal issue or double-issue *and* as a "separate" hardbound monograph. (This is a format which we also call a "DocuSerial.")

"Separates" are published because specialized libraries or professionals may wish to purchase a specific thematic issue by itself in a format which can be separately cataloged and shelved, as opposed to purchasing the journal on an on-going basis. Faculty members may also more easily consider a "separate" for classroom adoption.

"Separates" are carefully classified separately with the major book jobbers so that the journal tie-in can be noted on new book order slips to avoid duplicate purchasing.

You may wish to visit Haworth's website at . . .

http://www.HaworthPress.com

. . . to search our online catalog for complete tables of contents of these separates and related publications.

You may also call 1-800-HAWORTH (outside US/Canada: 607-722-5857), or Fax 1-800-895-0582 (outside US/Canada: 607-771-0012), or e-mail at:

docdelivery@haworthpress.com

Relationship Therapy with Same-Sex Couples, edited by Jerry J. Bigner, PhD, and Joseph L. Wetchler, PhD (Vol. 3, No. 2/3, 2004). *"A WINNER. Bigner and Wetchler have brought together all of the most current information on the dynamics of same-sex relationships in American society. Nowhere in the literature is this addressed so comprehensively. This is A MUST-READ for every couples counselor, every LGBTQQI counselor, and every counselor, period, for the insights and practical interventions that are offered throughout this invaluable book. The chapter authors offer important and thought-provoking insights into rarely explored subjects such as bisexual as well as transgender issues in same-sex couple therapy. EACH CHAPTER IS A GEM."* (Mark Pope, EdD, President, American Counseling Association [2003-2004]; Associate Professor, Division of Counseling & Family Therapy, University of Missouri-St. Louis)

Clinical Issues with Interracial Couples: Theories and Research, edited by Volker Thomas, PhD, Terri A. Karis, PhD, and Joseph L. Wetchler, PhD (Vol. 2, No. 2/3, 2003). *"A USEFUL TEXT IN FAMILY SYSTEMS AND THERAPY COURSES. . . . A very useful, and even necessary, text for clinicians who do couples work and will increasingly be dealing with cross-cultural and interracial couples."* (Maria P. P. Root, PhD, Psychologist, Seattle, Washington)

Couples, Intimacy Issues, and Addiction, edited by Barbara Jo Brothers, MSW, BCD, CGP (Vol. 10, No. 3/4, 2001).* *"A much needed and insightful book for those who already work with couples, and a marvelous addition to the library of any new therapist just venturing into the field of couples therapy. This book opens windows to explore, with respect and understanding, the many ways of partnering."* (Mary Ellen O'Hare-Lavin, PhD, Clinical Psychologist, Private Practice; Adjunct Faculty, Oakton Community College, Des Plaines, Illinois)

Couples and Body Therapy, edited by Barbara Jo Brothers, MSW, BCD, CGP (Vol. 10, No. 2, 2001).* *"A wonderful revisiting and blending of two significant fields. Once digested, one wonders how the therapist can focus on the couple without addressing the bodies they inhabit."* (Cindy Ashkins, PhD, LCSW, LMT, Couples Psychotherapist and Licensed Bodyworker in Private Practice, Metairie, North Carolina)

The Abuse of Men: Trauma Begets Trauma, edited by Barbara Jo Brothers, MSW, BCSW (Vol. 10, No. 1, 2001).* *"Addresses a topic that has been neglected. . . . This book is unique in adopting a systematic perspective that focuses not solely on the males who have been abused but also on their partners and family members. . . . Gives detailed and specific directions for intervening with couples who have experienced multiple traumas."* (Joseph A. Micucci, PhD, Associate Professor of Psychology, Chestnut Hill College, Pennsylvania)

The Personhood of the Therapist, edited by Barbara Jo Brothers, MSW, BCSW (Vol. 9, No. 3/4, 2000).* *Through suggestions, techniques, examples, and case studies, this book will help you develop a great sense of openness about yourself and your feelings, enabling you to offer clients more effective services.*

Couples Connecting: Prerequisites of Intimacy, edited by Barbara Jo Brothers, MSW, BCSW (Vol. 9, No. 1/2, 2000).* *"Brothers views marriage as an ideal context for the psychological and spiritual evolution of human beings, and invites therapists to reflect on the role they can play in facilitating this. Readers are sure to recognize their clients among the examples given and to return to their work with a renewed vision of the possibilities for growth and change." (Eleanor D. Macklin, PhD, Emeritus Professor and former Director of the Marriage and Family Therapy program, Syracuse University, New York)*

Couples Therapy in Managed Care: Facing the Crisis, edited by Barbara Jo Brothers, MSW, BCSW (Vol. 8, No. 3/4, 1999).* *Provides social workers, psychologists, and counselors with an overview of the negative effects of the managed care industry on the quality of mental health care. Within this book, you will discover the paradoxes that occur with the mixing of business principles and service principles and find valuable suggestions on how you can creatively cope within the managed care context. With* Couples Therapy in Managed Care, *you will learn how you can remain true to your own integrity and still get paid for your work and offer quality services within the current context of managed care.*

Couples and Pregnancy: Welcome, Unwelcome, and In-Between, edited by Barbara Jo Brothers, MSW, BCSW (Vol. 8, No. 2, 1999).* *Gain valuable insight into how pregnancy and birth have a profound psychological effect on the parents' relationship, especially on their experience of intimacy.*

Couples, Trauma, and Catastrophes, edited by Barbara Jo Brothers, MSW, BCSW (Vol. 7, No. 4, 1998).* *Helps therapists and counselors working with couples facing major crises and trauma.*

Couples: A Medley of Models, edited by Barbara Jo Brothers, MSW, BCSW, BCD (Vol. 7, No. 2/3, 1998).* *"A wonderful set of authors who illuminate different corners of relationships. This book belongs on your shelf . . . but only after you've read it and loved it." (Derek Paar, PhD, Associate Professor of Psychology, Springfield College, Massachusetts)*

When One Partner Is Willing and the Other Is Not, edited by Barbara Jo Brothers, MSW, BCSW (Vol. 7, No. 1, 1997).* *"An engaging variety of insightful perspectives on resistance in couples therapy." (Stan Taubman, DSW, Director of Managed Care, Alameda County Behavioral Health Care Service, Berkeley, California; Author,* Ending the Struggle Against Yourself)

Couples and the Tao of Congruence, edited by Barbara Jo Brothers, MSW, BCSW (Vol. 6, No. 3/4, 1996).* *"A library of information linking Virginia Satir's teaching and practice of creative improvement in human relations and the Tao of Congruence. . . . A stimulating read." (Josephine A. Bates, DSW, BD, retired mental health researcher and family counselor, Lake Preston, South Dakota)*

Couples and Change, edited by Barbara Jo Brothers, MSW, BCSW (Vol. 6, No. 1/2, 1996).* *This enlightening book presents readers with Satir's observations–observations that show the difference between thinking with systems in mind and thinking linearly–of process, interrelatedness, and attitudes.*

Couples: Building Bridges, edited by Barbara Jo Brothers, MSW, BCSW (Vol. 5, No. 4, 1996).* *"This work should be included in the library of anyone considering to be a therapist or who is one or who is fascinated by the terminology and conceptualizations which the study of marriage utilizes." (Irv Loev, PhD, MSW-ACP, LPC, LMFT, private practitioner)*

Couples and Countertransference, edited by Barbara Jo Brothers, MSW, BCSW (Vol. 5, No. 3, 1995).* *"I would recommend this book to beginning and advanced couple therapists as well as to social workers and psychologists. . . . This book is a wealth of information." (International Transactional Analysis Association)*

Power and Partnering, edited by Barbara Jo Brothers, MSW, BCSW (Vol. 5, No. 1/2, 1995).* *"Appeals to therapists and lay people who find themselves drawn to the works of Virginia Satir and Carl Jung. Includes stories and research data satisfying the tastes of both left- and right-brained readers." (Virginia O. Felder, ThM, Licensed Marriage and Family Therapist, private practice, Atlanta, Georgia)*

Surpassing Threats and Rewards: Newer Plateaus for Couples and Coupling, edited by Barbara Jo Brothers, MSW, BCSW (Vol. 4, No. 3/4, 1995).* *Explores the dynamics of discord, rejection, and blame in the coupling process and provides practical information to help readers understand marital dissatisfaction and how this dissatisfaction manifests itself in relationships.*

Attraction and Attachment: Understanding Styles of Relationships, edited by Barbara Jo Brothers, MSW, BCSW (Vol. 4, No. 1/2, 1994).* *"Ideas on working effectively with couples. . . . I strongly recommend this book for those who want to have a better understanding of the complex dynamics of couples and couples therapy." (Gilbert J. Greene, PhD, ACSW, Associate Professor, College of Social Work, The Ohio State University)*

Peace, War, and Mental Health: Couples Therapists Look at the Dynamics, edited by Barbara Jo Brothers, MSW, BCSW (Vol. 3, No. 4, 1993).* *Discover how issues of world war and peace relate to the dynamics of couples therapy in this thought-provoking book.*

Couples Therapy, Multiple Perspectives: In Search of Universal Threads, edited by Barbara Jo Brothers, MSW, BCSW (Vol. 3, No. 2/3, 1993).* *"A very sizeable team of couples therapists has scoured the countryside in search of the most effective methods for helping couples improve their relationships. . . . The bibliographies are a treasury of worthwhile references." (John F. Sullivan, EdS, Marriage and Family Counselor in Private Practice, Newburgh, New York)*

Spirituality and Couples: Heart and Soul in the Therapy Process, edited by Barbara Jo Brothers, MSW, BCSW (Vol. 3, No. 1, 1993).* *"Provides an array of reflections particularly for therapists beginning to address spirituality in the therapeutic process." (Journal of Family Psychotherapy)*

Equal Partnering: A Feminine Perspective, edited by Barbara Jo Brothers, MSW, BCSW (Vol. 2, No. 4, 1992).* *Designed to help couples, married or not, understand how to achieve a balanced, equal partnership.*

Coupling . . . What Makes Permanence? edited by Barbara Jo Brothers, MSW, BCSW (Vol. 2, No. 3, 1991).* *"Explores what it is that makes for a relationship in which each partner can grow and develop while remaining attached to another." (The British Journal of Psychiatry)*

Virginia Satir: Foundational Ideas, edited by Barbara Jo Brothers, MSW, BCSW (Vol. 2, No. 1/2, 1991).* *"The most thorough conglomeration of her ideas available today. Done in the intimate, yet clear fashion you would expect from Satir herself. . . . Well worth getting your hands damp to pick up this unique collection." (Journal of Family Psychotherapy)*

Intimate Autonomy: Autonomous Intimacy, edited by Barbara Jo Brothers, MSW, BCSW (Vol. 1, No. 3/4, 1991).* *"A fine collection of chapters on one of the most difficult of human tasks–getting close enough to another to share the warmth and benefits of that closeness without losing what is precious in our separations." (Howard Halpern, PhD, Author,* How to Break Your Addiction to a Person)

Couples on Coupling, edited by Barbara Jo Brothers, MSW, BCSW (Vol. 1, No. 2, 1990).* *"A variety of lenses through which to view relationships, each providing a different angle for seeing patterns, strengths, and problems and for gaining insight into a given couple system." (Suzanne Imes, PhD, Clinical Psychologist, Private Practice, Atlanta, Georgia; Adjunct Assistant Professor of Psychology, Georgia State University)*

Relationship Therapy with Same-Sex Couples

Jerry J. Bigner , PhD
Joseph L. Wetchler, PhD
Editors

Relationship Therapy with Same-Sex Couples has been co-published si-multaneously as *Journal of Couple & Relationship Therapy*, Volume 3, Numbers 2/3 2004.

The Haworth Press, Inc.

New York • London • Victoria (AU)
www.HaworthPress.com

Relationship Therapy with Same-Sex Couples has been co-published simultaneously as *Journal of Couple & Relationship Therapy*™, Volume 3, Numbers 2/3 2004.

Cover design by Jennifer M. Gaska

Library of Congress Cataloging-in-Publication Data

Relationship therapy with same-sex couples/ [edited by] Jerry J. Bigner, Joseph L. Wetchler.
    p. cm.
    Published also as v. 3, no. 2/3, 2004, of the Journal of couple & relationship therapy.
    Includes bibliographical references and index.
    ISBN 0-7890-2554-X (hard cover : alk. paper) – ISBN 0-7890-2555-8 (soft cover : alk paper)
    1. Gay couples–Psychology. 2. Counseling. I. Bigner, Jerry J. II. Wetchler, Joseph L. III. Journal of couple & relationship therapy.
HQ76.34.R45 2004
306.84'8–dc22

2004017774

Indexing, Abstracting & Website/Internet Coverage

This section provides you with a list of major indexing & abstracting services and other tools for bibliographic access. That is to say, each service began covering this periodical during the year noted in the right column. Most Websites which are listed below have indicated that they will either post, disseminate, compile, archive, cite or alert their own Website users with research-based content from this work. (This list is as current as the copyright date of this publication.)

(continued)

*Exact start date to come.

Special Bibliographic Notes related to special journal issues (separates) and indexing/abstracting:

- indexing/abstracting services in this list will also cover material in any "separate" that is co-published simultaneously with Haworth's special thematic journal issue or DocuSerial. Indexing/abstracting usually covers material at the article/chapter level.
- monographic co-editions are intended for either non-subscribers or libraries which intend to purchase a second copy for their circulating collections.
- monographic co-editions are reported to all jobbers/wholesalers/approval plans. The source journal is listed as the "series" to assist the prevention of duplicate purchasing in the same manner utilized for books-in-series.
- to facilitate user/access services all indexing/abstracting services are encouraged to utilize the co-indexing entry note indicated at the bottom of the first page of each article/chapter/contribution.
- this is intended to assist a library user of any reference tool (whether print, electronic, online, or CD-ROM) to locate the monographic version if the library has purchased this version but not a subscription to the source journal.
- individual articles/chapters in any Haworth publication are also available through the Haworth Document Delivery Service (HDDS).

Relationship Therapy
with Same-Sex Couples

CONTENTS

ABOUT THE EDITORS

Jerry J. Bigner, PhD, is Professor Emeritus in the Department of Human Development and Family Studies at Colorado State University. He is a Research Member of the American Family Therapy Academy and a member of the National Council on Family Relations. He is the editor of the *Journal of GLBT Family Studies* and serves on the Editorial Board of the *Journal of Couple & Relationship Therapy*. He is a reviewer for *Family Relations*. He has had clinical experience leading to the Marriage and Family Therapy license in Colorado and has worked with gay and lesbian clientele. He is the author of *Parent-Child Relations*, now in its seventh edition, and has authored two life span development texts. His main research areas focus on gay and lesbian parenting and therapeutic issues relating to gay and lesbian families. He has numerous research publications as well as chapters in texts on these topics. He also has provided expert witness testimony on behalf of gay and lesbian parents and for the Canadian same-sex marriage litigation. Dr. Bigner is co-editor with Dr. Joe Wetchler of the forthcoming *Working with Same-Sex Couples,* and is the editor of the forthcoming *GLBT Family Studies: Introduction and Future Trends.*

Joseph L. Wetchler, PhD, is Professor of Marriage and Family Therapy, and Director of the Master's Program in the Marriage and Family Therapy Program at Purdue University Calumet. He is a Clinical Member and Approved Supervisor of the American Association for Marriage and Family Therapy. Dr. Wetchler was the recipient of the *1997 IAMFT Award for Outstanding Contribution to Research in Family Life.* He is the Editor of the *Journal of Couple & Relationship Therapy,* and has served on the Editoral Boards of *the American Journal of Family Therapy,* the *Journal of Family Psychotherapy,* the *Journal of Feminist Family Therapy,* the *Journal of Marital and Family Therapy,* and the *Journal of Activities in Psychotherapy Practice.* Dr. Wetchler is a co-editor (with Lorna Hecker) of *An Introduction to Marriage and Family Therapy* and a co-author (with Fred Piercy & Douglas Sprenkle) of the *Family Therapy Sourcebook 2nd ed.* He is also the author of numerous journal articles on family therapy supervision, family therapy for child and adolescent problems, family therapy for substance abuse, couple therapy, and the self of the therapist. Dr. Wetchler has been a co-investigator on a large project funded by the National Institute on Drug Abuse to study couple therapy approaches for substance abusing women. He regularly consults to social service agencies and therapists in private practice, and maintains an active family therapy practice in Northwest Indiana. Dr. Wetchler is a licensed marriage and family therapist in Indiana.

Foreword

For same-sex couples, the political and psychological are inseparable, and the year 2003 has been filled with unparalleled political paradoxes. Witness the following:

- The United States Supreme Court ruled that state laws criminalizing homosexual sex between consenting adults (the so-called "sodomy laws") were unconstitutional. Adults who engage in homosexual relations are no longer outlaws.
- Because they claim that legal recognition of same-sex relationships will destroy the American family, a group of conservative religious and political leaders have started a movement for an amendment to the U.S. constitution to prohibit marriage and any of the legal components of marriage for same-sex couples. If such a constitutional amendment were passed, same-sex couples would have no legal recourse in the courts or elsewhere to obtain marriage or any other couple rights except through another amendment to the constitution.
- The State of California, which in an earlier ballot initiative banned the recognition of same-sex marriages, enacted domestic partners legislation conferring on same-sex couples most of the major privileges and obligations of heterosexual marriage.
- Canada enacted laws permitting same-sex marriage.
- Taiwan became the first country in Asia to formally consider laws allowing marriage and child adoption by same-sex couples.

Robert-Jay Green is Professor and Associate Director, Clinical Psychology PhD Program, California School of Professional Psychology, Alliant International University-San Francisco Campus.

Address correspondence to: Robert-Jay Green, PhD, Professor and Associate Director, Clinical Psychology PhD Program, California School of Professional Psychology, Alliant International University, 1 Beach Street, San Francisco, CA 94133 (E-mail: rjgreen@alliant.edu).

[Haworth co-indexing entry note]: "Foreword." Green, Robert-Jay. Co-published simultaneously in *Journal of Couple & Relationship Therapy* (The Haworth Press) Vol. 3, No. 2/3, 2004, pp.xix-xxiii; and: *Relationship Therapy with Same-Sex Couples* (ed: Jerry J. Bigner, and Joseph L. Wetchler) The Haworth Press, Inc., 2004, pp. xiii-xvii. Single or multiple copies of this article are available for a fee from The Haworth Document Delivery Service [1-800-HAWORTH, 9:00 a.m. - 5:00 p.m. (EST). E-mail address: docdelivery@haworthpress.com].

http://www.haworthpress.com/web/JCRT

- Although the Massachusetts Supreme Court seems reasonably likely to rule in favor of same-sex marriages later this year, other U.S. states during the past year (as did the federal government a couple of years ago) passed laws banning recognition of same-sex marriages performed anywhere (the so-called "defense of marriage" state laws).
- Public opinion polls continued to suggest that a majority of the American public is strongly against granting same-sex couples the right to marry. However, when asked about particular rights, a majority of those polled are in favor of granting many of the specific privileges of marriages to same-sex couples (i.e., inheritance rights, partner insurance benefits, hospital visitation privileges, health care power of attorney rights, social security benefits for surviving partners).

This paradoxical social context–made up of persistent antigay prejudice, mixed public support for some same-sex relationship benefits, anti-gay marriage legislative initiatives, and significant progress in the courts and in selected states–tends to be internalized to varying degrees by all GLBT persons. Although most same-sex partners are able to cope successfully with the special challenges they face and do not need professional help in order to do so (Gottman, Levenson, Swanson, Swanson, Tyson, & Yoshimoto, D., 2003; Gottman, Levenson, Gross, Frederickson, McCoy, Rosenthal, Ruef, & Yoshimoto, 2003; Green, Bettinger, & Zacks, 1996), there still are many same-sex partners who are unable to resist the negative cultural messages and thus are more likely to have couple problems related to being gay, lesbian, bisexual, or transgendered.

Elsewhere (Green & Mitchell, 2002), I have proposed that all same-sex couples face a similar set of challenges: (1) coping with homophobia and heterosexism in the larger society; (2) maintaining a sense of couplehood despite the lack of a normative/legal template for same-sex relationships; (3) creating social networks that provide emotional support and family-like interconnections among network members; and (4) maintaining flexible gender roles (androgyny) and avoiding the increased risks of emotional fusion and over-dependency in female couples, or emotional disengagement and competition in male couples, which accompany traditional gender role conformity.

A general framework for treating these types of GLBT-specific couple problems is presented in Table 1 (p. xvii). Although space limitations preclude a fuller description here, previous articles have discussed relationship dynamics and interventions in depth (Green et al., 1996; Green & Mitchell, 2002). Moreover, I believe it is important for readers to keep in mind here and throughout this volume that homosexuality and heterosexuality are not opposites. Rather, they are variations on a single theme of human romantic attachments, sexual attraction, and the capacity for love. Most of the problems that same-sex couples present for therapy are identical to the problems presented by heterosexual couples–communication problems; difficulties in managing conflicts and anger; sexual dysfunctions and lack of desire; feeling lonely and disconnected in the relationship; problems with in-laws; arguments over money, work, and sometimes childrearing; and problems related to secrecy and lying about sexual and/or romantic connections outside of the couple relationship.

None of these problems is unique to a group of couples as a function of their sexual orientation. Much of the therapeutic work with same-sex couples is identical to work with heterosexual couples. It thus behooves therapists who work with GLBT populations to get specific training and supervision in couple therapy and not assume that their general training in psychotherapy or expertise in GLBT mental health prepares them to do therapy with same-sex

TABLE 1. Challenges Faced by Same-Sex Couples and Their Implications for Problem Development and Treatment

CHALLENGES	Potential Couple Problems	Therapeutic Interventions	Outcome Goals
(1) Homophobia and Heterosexism in the Community and Larger Society	Internalized Homophobia–Fear and Ambivalence About Committing to a Same-Sex Couple Relationship	Externalizing the Problem (Viewing Societal Ignorance and Prejudice–Not Homosexuality–as the Problem)	Self-Acceptance of GLBT Identity; Ability to Commit to a Same-Sex Relationship Without Fear, Guilt, or Ambivalence
(2) Lack of Normative and Legal Template for Same-Sex Couplehood	Relational Ambiguity (Unclear Couple Commitment, Boundaries, Expectations, and Obligations); Anxious/Dependent or Avoidant/Dismissive Attachment	Exploration and Collaboration About What Being a Couple Means to Them (Vows, Roles, Boundaries, Expectations, and Obligations)	Commitment Clarity, Operating as Team, Primary Commitment to Each Other, Longer-Term Planning Ability, Secure Attachment
(3) Generally Lower Levels of Family Support, and Less Social Network Cohesion	Social Isolation; Lack of Couple Identity in a Defined Community; Inability to Get Emotional Support, Advice, and Instrumental Help from a Support System When Needed	Coaching to Build "Families of Choice" (Cohesive Social Support Networks with Interconnections Among Network Members)	Embedded Couple Identity & Sense of Community of Care (Social Network Cohesion, Reciprocity of Support, Higher Levels of Emotional and Instrumental Support)
(4) Same-Sex Composition of Couple Increases Likelihood of Certain Kind of Problems if Both Partners Conform to Traditional Gender Roles Rather than Being Androgynous	Problems of Emotional Fusion and Avoidance of Conflict in Female Couples Problems of Emotional Disengagement or Competition in Male Couples	Deconstructing the Partners' Traditional Male or Female Gender Socialization; Encouraging Resistance and Subversion of Conventional Gender Role Conformity in the Relationship	Androgynous, Flexible, Egalitarian Sharing of Emotional and Instrumental Roles in the Couple's Relationship; Collaborative Rather than Avoidant or Competitive Approach to Conflict Resolution

couples. Likewise, surveys show that about half of all couple and family therapists do not feel sufficiently prepared to work with GLBT clients in therapy (Doherty & Simmons, 1996). A key task of the therapist is to be able to distinguish when a same-sex couple's presenting problems are related to GLBT-specific challenges as described in Table 1 as opposed to generic couple processes such as communication, conflict management, or common attachment problems. Couple therapists face the twin dangers of over-attributing or under-attributing a couple's problems to GLBT causal factors. In order to make this kind of accurate differential assessment, a therapist optimally should have significant expertise in both couple therapy and GLBT issues, or should receive relevant ongoing consultation for same-sex couple therapy cases.

To help increase the field's knowledge base in this regard, *Relationship Therapy with Same-Sex Couples* represents a major milestone in publications about same-sex couples. Although many excellent articles have been written about same-sex couples as well as a recent outstanding book on gay male couples in therapy (Greenan & Tunnell, 2002), no other publication covers the variety of couple types (gay, lesbian, bisexual, mixed orientation, transgender), specific treatment foci (sex therapy, coparenting, multi-cultural issues), and training issues (straight therapists, supervision issues, resources) as is represented here. Having spent a lot of my professional life contemplating these very matters and feeling that there was "nothing new under the sun" in most of what I have been reading lately, I was very excited to find so many new ideas in *Relationship Therapy with Same-Sex Couples*. Many thanks to co-editors Jerry Bigner, Joseph Wetchler, and the distinguished contributing authors for this insightful work. It is destined to become a classic in our field.

Robert-Jay Green

REFERENCES

Doherty, W. J., & Simmons, D. S. (1996). Clinical practice patterns of marriage and family therapists: A national survey of therapists and their clients. *Journal of Marital & Family Therapy, 22,* 9-5.

Gottman, J. M, Levenson, R. W., Swanson, C., Swanson, K., Tyson, R., Yoshimoto, D. (2003). Observing gay, lesbian and heterosexual couple's relationships: Mathematical modeling of conflict interaction. *Journal of Homosexuality, 45,* 65-91.

Gottman, J. M., Levenson, R. W., Gross, J., Frederickson, B. L., McCoy, K., Rosenthal, L., Ruef, A., & Yoshimoto, D. (2003). Correlates of gay and lesbian couple's relationship satisfaction and relationship dissolution. *Journal of Homosexuality, 45,* 23-43.

Green, R-J., Bettinger, M., & Zacks, E. (1996). Are lesbian couples fused and gay male couples disengaged?: Questioning gender straightjackets. In J. Laird & R-J. Green (Eds.), *Lesbians and gays in couples and families: A handbook for therapists* (pp. 185-230). San Francisco: Jossey-Bass (a division of Wiley).

Green, R.-J., & Mitchell, V. (2002). Gay and lesbian couples in therapy: Homophobia, relational ambiguity, and social support. In A.S. Gurman & N.S. Jacobson (Eds.), *Clinical handbook of couple therapy (3rd ed.)* (pp. 546-568). New York: Guilford Press.

Greenan, D., & Tunnell, G. (2002). *Couples therapy with gay men.* New York: Guilford Press.

Hartman, A. (1996). Social policy as a context for lesbian and gay families: The political is personal. In J. Laird & R-J. Green (Eds.), *Lesbians and gays in couples and families: A handbook for therapists* (pp. 69-85). San Francisco: Jossey-Bass.

Acknowledgements

This text represents a number of things for me. First, it is my swan song of sorts as I (Jerry Bigner) am soon to retire (not altogether, I'm afraid) from a very active academic career. I wanted to do something that would make a statement about the issues and needs I believe in very strongly that affect GLBT individuals and their families. So, in many respects, this represents–an epic achievement in a long career of teaching, research, and service. It would not have happened, of course, without Joe Wetchler's support and solid backing. Joe is a gifted therapist and mentor beyond measure. Others like my partner Duane, my children (Todd, Julie, Shannon, Katy), and grandchildren (Lauren, Megan) continue to be a source of support and inspiration. The folks at Haworth Press have been incredibly supportive as well. And then there are the authors of the various chapters who have spoken from their experience as well as their hearts about issues they hold near and dear. Lastly, I wish to dedicate this text to all people of the GLBT communities, their families of origin, their families of choice, and their allies who take risks large and small everyday to make this a better place in which to live, love, and work.

No book exists in isolation. It evolves from both historical and present-centered contexts. I (Joe Wetchler) have been extremely lucky to work with an exceptional co-editor in Jerry Bigner. He has been a model of organization and collaboration. Further, the authors on this project were simply first rate. I am extremely grateful for their belief in this book and their willingness to produce some of the best chapters I have read on GLBT issues. I also want to thank Bill Cohen and Kathy Rutz of the Haworth Press for their support and their ideas. As always, I want to thank my wife Carole, my parents Bernie and Jorie, my sisters Diane and Sherry, my stepchildren Ryan and Jessica Marie, and my daughter Jessica Lily for their love and positive strokes. Finally, I want to dedicate this book to Wally, Sherry, and Julie for their inspiration.

Jerry J. Bigner
Joseph L. Wetchler
Editors

[Haworth co-indexing entry note]: "Acknowledgements." Wetchler, Joseph L. Co-published simultaneously in *Journal of Couple & Relationship Therapy* (The Haworth Press) Vol. 3, No. 2/3, 2004, pp. xxv; and: *Relationship Therapy with Same-Sex Couples* (ed: Jerry J. Bigner, and Joseph L. Wetchler) The Haworth Press, Inc., 2004, pp. xix. Single or multiple copies of this article are available for a fee from The Haworth Document Delivery Service [1-800-HAWORTH, 9:00 a.m. - 5:00 p.m. (EST). E-mail address: docdelivery@haworthpress.com].

Introduction

We are often asked by both beginning and experienced therapists for assistance and supervision in working with gay, lesbian, bisexual, and transgender (GLBT) individuals, couples, and families. Although this is not unusual, we have been impressed with how little formal training as well as direct experience most therapists have in working with this special population of clients. This became especially clear to Jerry one day not long ago when he was discussing a fairly uncomplicated clinical case with a graduate student. As the two worked through the various questions the student had about the gay male couple who were having problems with communication, Jerry asked a clarification question to be sure he understood the point he had been making about how two gay men in relationship may settle conflicts. The student's reply was to ask a question of Jerry: "Then which one (of these men) is the woman?" Thus, the need for a special volume on working with same-sex couples became even more crystal clear, especially in this more enlightened day and age.

Most of us, in learning to be therapists, must ultimately confront ourselves to better understand the clients we treat. This reality is much more concrete in the case of therapists who have GLBT clients. It is with this group of people that therapists come face-to-face with the stereotypes, misconceptions, and irrationalities that our society traditionally teaches about homosexuality and those who belong to sexual minorities. Ignorance and lack of experience often are the breeding ground for misunderstanding clients, which may stem from inadequate training or the incorrect belief that GLBT clients do not seek nor need therapeutic assistance in their relationships. This also may occur because GLBT clients perhaps shy away from anyone, or any agency, that includes "marriage" in their title because of the perception that these cater primarily to heterosexuals.

Jerry J. Bigner, PhD, is Professor Emeritas, Department of Human Development and Family Studies, Colorado State University, Fort Collins, CO 80523.

Joseph L. Wetchler, PhD, is Professor, and Program Director, Marriage and Family Therapy Program, Purdue University Calumet, Hammond, IN 46323.

[Haworth co-indexing entry note]: "Introduction." Bigner, Jerry J., and Joseph L. Wetchler. Co-published simultaneously in *Journal of Couple & Relationship Therapy* (The Haworth Press) Vol. 3, No. 2/3, 2004, pp. 1-2; and: *Relationship Therapy with Same-Sex Couples* (ed: Jerry J. Bigner, and Joseph L. Wetchler) The Haworth Press, Inc., 2004, pp. 1-2. Single or multiple copies of this article are available for a fee from The Haworth Document Delivery Service [1-800-HAWORTH, 9:00 a.m. - 5:00 p.m. (EST). E-mail address: docdelivery@haworthpress.com].

http://www.haworthpress.com/web/JCRT
Digital Object Identifier: 10.1300/J398v03n02_01

The American Psychiatric Association and the American Psychological Association, as well as other professional groups, have discarded the notion that homosexuality itself is a mental illness. However, there continues to be a lack of emphasis in many therapeutic training programs on preparing therapists to work with GLBT clients, especially in their intimate relationships. Thus, we have tried in this collection to present manuscripts by therapists working with the gamut of issues particular to GLBT individuals, couples, and their families. Some of these topics are rarely addressed even in the training programs that include GLBT issues such as those experienced by spouses and ex-spouses, families of individuals planning sex-reassignment surgery, and those who are bisexual. Further, this publication was prepared not only for beginning therapists but also for those more experienced who seek to widen their therapeutic wisdom.

Jerry J. Bigner
Joseph L. Wetchler

Clinical Issues with Same-Sex Couples: A Review of the Literature

Colleen M. Connolly

SUMMARY. While universal issues exist for all couples, same-sex couples present distinct clinical concerns that impact relational health. After reviewing the current literature in the field, two major issues emerged as significant: societal oppression and relational issues distinctive to same-sex gay, lesbian, and bisexual couples. Societal oppression includes homophobia, heterosexism, and the internalization of these dynamics. Additionally, the "coming out" process and gender role socialization uniquely impact the same-sex couple. Other areas that therapists need to consider when working with this population include multiple cultural variables, dyadic stage-related issues, and the couple's negotiation and maintenance of "family." *[Article copies available for a fee from The Haworth Document Delivery Service: 1-800-HAWORTH. E-mail address: <docdelivery@haworth press.com> Website: <http://www.HaworthPress.com> © 2004 by The Haworth Press, Inc. All rights reserved.]*

Colleen M. Connolly is Assistant Professor, Southwest Texas State University, EAPS/Education Building 4016, 606 University Drive, San Marcos, TX 78666.

[Haworth co-indexing entry note]: "Clinical Issues with Same-Sex Couples: A Review of the Literature." Connolly, Colleen M. Co-published simultaneously in *Journal of Couple & Relationship Therapy* (The Haworth Press) Vol. 3, No. 2/3, 2004, pp. 3-12; and: *Relationship Therapy with Same-Sex Couples* (ed: Jerry J. Bigner, and Joseph L. Wetchler) The Haworth Press, Inc., 2004, pp. 3-12. Single or multiple copies of this article are available for a fee from The Haworth Document Delivery Service [1-800-HAWORTH, 9:00 a.m. - 5:00 p.m. (EST). E-mail address: docdelivery@haworthpress.com].

http://www.haworthpress.com/web/JCRT
Digital Object Identifier: 10.1300/J398v03n02_02

3

KEYWORDS. Same-sex couples, oppression, gay, lesbian, homophobia, heterosexism, coming out, gender role socialization, couple stages, maintaining family

Same-sex couples seek therapy for issues that are universal to all couples, such as communication problems, infidelity, substance abuse, and decision-making about staying together or separating (Cabaj & Klinger, 1996). However, the predominant issues that distinguish gay, lesbian, and bisexual same-sex (GLB) couples from heterosexual opposite-sex couples are the impact of gender role socialization and the societal oppression generalized as homophobia and heterosexism. I say "generalized" because the very existence of homophobia (Brown, 1995; Granvold & Martin, 1999; Ossana, 2000; Slater, 1995) and heterosexism (Brown, 1995; Granvold & Martin, 1999; Ossana, 2000; Reynolds & Hanjorgiris, 2000; Slater, 1995) lead to a multitude of couple stressors, including internalized homophobia (Brown, 1988; Cabaj & Klinger, 1996; Falco, 1996; Shernoff, 1995; Slater & Mencher, 1991; Slater, 1995).

Similarities and differences also exist among the same-sex GLB couple population. Parallels include being forced to make decisions about keeping their couplehood hidden or lifting the mask and revealing their identity (Goldenberg & Goldenberg, 1998). Couples also must evaluate if it is safe or wise to disclose (Scrivner & Eldridge, 1995) in the social, familial, and professional arenas.

The differences are mainly two-fold. First, our culture historically has diverse reactions to males who are gay or bisexual and females who are lesbian or bisexual, with a much more negative reaction to male-male interaction (Goldenberg & Goldenberg, 1998). Second, most GLB individuals grow up in a heterosexual-based family of origin (Slater, 1995), and role models for same-sex couples have been considered limited (Young & Long, 1998), lacking (Ossana, 2000), and absent (Falco, 1996). Same-sex couples must manage major life transitions, as in creating, transitioning, or dissolving their relationship (Granvold & Martin, 1999), while experiencing a deficiency in normative support systems or rituals (Slater, 1995).

The purpose of this article is to summarize the most predominant clinical issues when working with same-sex couples. Two external factors of primary importance, cultural oppression and the impact of gender role socialization (Brown, 1995), will be reviewed. I will then highlight how these repressive features can affect and distress the same-sex relational dyad.

SOCIETAL OPPRESSION

A pivotal clinical issue with same-sex couples is cultural oppression, with heterosexism and homophobia–and the internalization of both–intruding into an individual's functioning and permeating the same-sex couple dynamic (Brown, 1995). Indeed, Brown (2000) suggests that all couples "function in the context of these two interlocking forms of oppression" (p. 275).

Homophobia

Societal homophobia takes many forms and can range from violence (Granvold & Martin, 1999; Ossana, 2000) and victimization (Dworkin, 2000) to everyday slights and slurs occurring in casual conversation (Davison, 2001). Homophobia is institutionalized (Simons, 1991) and legitimized by discriminating and denying the GLB population their intrinsic human and civil rights (Bigner, 2000).

This homophobia extends to a lack of legal recognition and protection for same-sex partners and their families (Ossana, 2000; Young & Long, 1998). Legislated homophobia, reflected in the absence of legal protection, can result in a couple's marginalization or loss in a variety of areas: child custody rights (Ossana, 2000; Shernoff, 1995; Slater, 1995), important medical decision-making power for the partner (Ossana, 2000), employment (Granvold & Martin, 1999; Slater, 1995), shelter (Slater, 1995; Slater & Mencher, 1991), health care, and in social services (Granvold & Martin, 1999).

Societal homophobia (Ossana, 2000; Reynolds & Hanjorgiris, 2000) is inherently discriminatory (Granvold & Martin, 1999; Ossana, 2000) hostile, and prejudicial (Ossana, 2000). The label "homoprejudice"–versus homophobia– appears to be a more precise representation (Logan, 1996); however, this term has not yet taken hold in the literature.

Heterosexism

Heterosexism, or the belief that an opposite-sex-based relationship is superior and preferable to a same-sex relationship, is oppressive (Bigner, 2000). Unfortunately, these ideas still linger in clinical practice theory models (Basham, 1999). However, they can take on a more subtle and insidious form (Bigner, 2000; Ossana, 2000). For example, couples do not see the media highlighting happy, satisfied, and successful same-sex couples. In addition, when the media does portray gay men and lesbian women, they appear as single individuals (Ossana, 2000). All people are influenced as these beliefs are "acquired, communicated, and reinforced throughout society over the entire life span of individuals" (Bigner, 2000, p. 279).

Internalized Homophobia

The enculturation of homophobia and heterosexism dramatically affects the GLB individual and couple. The internalized homophobia and biphobia (Dworkin, 2000) result in feelings of somehow being "defective" (Schiemann &

Smith, 1996). When homophobia is internalized it can result in self-hatred, guilt, and pessimism about the possibility of longevity in same-sex relationships (Ossana, 2000).

Couples might question the viability of the relationship, and the presumption that the relationship is temporary, platonic, or incidental undermines relational confidence (Slater & Mencher, 1991). Often a couple's faith in their bond is at risk (Slater, 1995). The therapist, who might be the only witness (Simmons, 1991) and historian (Schiemann & Smith, 1996) to their relationship, plays an important role in their life.

Time and again it becomes the couple's own task to verify and validate the relationship. The lack of external validation increases internalized homophobia (Slater & Mencher, 1991). Furthermore, this internalization process can have a tumultuous effect on dyadic functioning (Cabaj & Klinger, 1996) and contribute to difficulties in identity formation (Brown, 1988; Reynolds & Hanjorgiris, 2000), identity management (Reynolds & Hanjorgiris, 2000), and the "coming out" process (Cabaj & Klinger, 1996) as a GLB person.

The "Coming Out" Process

Invisibility is central to the functioning of homophobia (Simons, 1991) and heterosexism. The decision to come out as gay, lesbian (Ossana, 2000; Reynolds & Hanjorgiris, 2000) or bisexual (Dworkin, 2000) is more than an individual decision; it is also "a matter of couple identity, synchronism, and resource mobilization" (Patterson, Ciabattari, & Schwartz, 1999, p. 342).

On a more explicit level, same-sex couples frequently maintain multiple identities and expend extra energy safeguarding (Davison, 2001) and compartmentalizing different relationships in diverse environments. This confounding dynamic may lead to feelings of lack of power and control in separating "those who know" and "those who don't know" (Slater, 1995).

Implicitly, couples are denied the aid, comfort, and support heterosexuals frequently experience during times of crisis (Roth, 1985) and contend with a wide-range invisibility of milestones (Johnson & Colucci, 1999). So same-sex couples can be in a double bind: Do they endure the stresses of invisibility or risk the consequences of disclosure (Slater, 1995)? Another challenge lies in negotiating the private and public identity (Slater, 1995; Slater & Mencher, 1991) as couples frequently function in two separate and conflicting worlds (Slater, 1995).

Deciding not to come out can be based on fear. However, it may be a strategic choice that carries no hidden meanings about identity acceptance (Patterson, Ciabattari, & Schwartz, 1999). One important distinction might be, is the decision based on a perceived need to save "unnecessary pain" or on a persistent self-hatred (Shernoff, 1995, p. 912)?

Either way, revealing one's identity is a continual process (Falco, 1996) further complicated by gender and culture (Dworkin, 2000). To disclose heightens the risk of rejection and marginalization, whereas to not disclose may result in isolation and the "duress of leading a 'double life'" (p. 283) that lends itself to behaviors that invalidate the relationship (Ossana, 2000).

Gender Role Socialization

An additional area of distinction with same-sex GLB couples is the impact of gender role socialization (Brown, 1995; Cabaj & Klinger, 1996; Goldenberg & Goldenberg, 1998; Granvold & Martin, 1999; Johnson & Colucci, 1999; Ossana, 2000; Scrivner & Eldridge, 1995; Young & Long, 1998). All members of society are enculturated with gender norms. According to Brown (1995), both members of a same-sex couple "possess variations on the theme of the same benefits and deficits of essentially similar patterns of gender role development" (p. 274).

Scrivner and Eldridge (1995) identified three dyadic themes affected by gender role socialization: emotional intimacy, sexuality, and power. When approaching emotional intimacy, women are socialized to care and nurture. Men are more socially valued when expressing their autonomous and separate selves.

From a sexual expression framework, Scrivner and Eldridge contend that men generally are socialized to express the sexual before the emotional, whereas women prefer an affectional relationship before initiating the sexual aspect. Power, with the issue of equality versus power differential in couples (Scrivner & Eldridge, 1995), and power as demonstrated by financial resources and sharing (Johnson & Colucci, 1999) is impacted by our socialization as gendered males and females.

There are, of course, variations and exceptions to these concepts, but clearly society exerts social pressure through prejudice and gender socialization (Young & Long, 1998).

RELATIONAL ISSUES

Societal oppression may also affect the couples from a relational standpoint. These include cultural variables, stage-related issues, and the couple's maintenance and negotiation of family.

Cultural Variables

Same-sex partners frequently juggle multiple and diverse identity positions. Couples are often more dissimilar than opposite-sex couples in race (Young & Long, 1998; Patterson, Ciabattari, & Schwartz, 1999), ethnicity, socioeconomic position (Young & Long, 1998), age, and education (Patterson,

Ciabattari, & Schwartz, 1999). Moreover, GLB identity "has very different meanings in different racial or ethnic groups, accepted or tolerated in some and considered an abomination or even an impossibility in others" (Basham, 1999, p. 148). The GLB population is an incredibly diverse group drawn together by limitations in places to gather and meet (Patterson & Schwartz, 1994). The GLB identity is not always seen as primary (Johnson & Colucci, 1999), and couple conflict may ensue as a result of divided loyalties (Granvold & Martin, 1999) among orientation, culture, and family identity.

Stage-Related Issues

Three stage-related issues were summarized in the literature: partner differences in the coming out process, differing generational factors, and discrepancies in couple stage development. "Stages" of the coming out process frequently affect partners differently, and more typically than not, one partner within the couple is usually at a different stage from the other partner (Mattison & McWhirter, 1987; McWhirter & Mattison, 1996). The more "experienced" partner may worry if the relationship is transient; the less experienced partner may feel threatened by partner's degree of disclosure and involvement in the GLB community (Ossana, 2000).

An additional stage-related issue is the generational factor in which identity formation is variable and based on historical and sociopolitical contexts (Barón & Cramer, 2000). Ossana (2000) reflected on some possibilities in this regard. What was the societal attitude at the time of coming out? Was it before or after the GL liberation movement? Was the community conservative or liberal, rural or urban? What were family and peer reactions, including cultural and religious beliefs?

Additionally, the concept of relational stage discrepancy was identified as it related to male couples. Mattison and McWhirter (Mattison & McWhirter, 1987; McWhirter & Mattison, 1996) identified six developmental stages of relationship: blending, nesting, maintaining, building, releasing, and renewing. The authors suggest that a "stage discrepancy" occurs with frequency. For example, one partner may be in a comfortable position of maintaining the relationship while the other partner remains "dependent and clinging" (McWhirter & Mattison, 1996, p. 330).

While the stages may not be exact for female couples, stages do occur and discrepancies exist for these couples also. Without understanding the coming-out stage, generational-stage differences, or relational-stage discrepancy, same-sex couples often consider their difficulties as a personal or relational flaw rather than recognizing that differences are typically correctable or manageable by relational growth and development (Mattison & McWhirter, 1987; McWhirter & Mattison, 1996).

Negotiating and Maintaining "Family"

When addressing issues of family, same-sex couples perceive less support than married couples do (Patterson, Ciabattari, & Schwartz, 1999) and commonly lack extended family support, particularly if they are not out (Granvold & Martin, 1999).

Frequently family of origin has the assumption of heterosexuality, with expectations of an opposite-sex partner and children with that partner (Matthews & Lease, 2000). The dynamics of secrecy among "unchosen" families (Patterson, Ciabattari, & Schwartz, 1999, p. 341), such as those families that one is born, adopted, or fostered into, are frequently in full play.

Same-sex dyads also experience loss around the "heterosexual privilege" in their family of origin (Young & Long, 1998) and in the wider culture. It is not uncommon for a full-cycle grief process to exist for the entire family (Matthews & Lease, 2000).

Roth (1985), in identifying issues affecting female couples, suggests that family members and the heterosexual environment regularly invalidate the same-sex couple. This invalidation repeatedly leads couples to seek therapy early in the development of their relationship.

Some couples experience bond-invalidating activities, such as rendering the relationship invisible or acting as if the relationship exists but then disqualifying it as "not genuine" or "a stage" (Roth, 1985, p. 276). At other times, the couple's relationship is directly invaded, such as excluding the partner in holidays and family rituals, or giving separate rooms when visiting (Roth, 1985).

Often an unwillingness exists in accepting the same-sex couple as a legitimate union (Granvold & Martin, 1999), with families and others actually undermining the relationship (Brown, 1988). Families and the heterosexually-bound world over and over again treat a partnered member either as single (Brown, 1995; Granvold & Martin, 1999) or as a perpetual adolescent (McGoldrick, 1989), who is expected to return home without their partner (Brown, 1988).

However, the recognition among the therapeutic community that "family" for the GLB population can either be chosen (Granvold & Martin, 1999; Patterson, Ciabattari, & Schwartz, 1999) or created (Granvold & Martin, 1999) has come to the forefront. Therefore, there can be structured alternatives in "chosen" families and communities (Patterson, Ciabattari, & Schwartz, 1999). The process of negotiating and maintaining family requires overtly- or covertly-made decisions about who family might be, and some couples need therapeutic intervention to expand their circle of support.

CONCLUSION

Blurred lines remain in discerning whether an issue is relationally based or generated by external stressors associated with a GLB identity (Brown, 1995). Normal life stage dilemmas are complicated by oppressive cultural biases (Brown, 1988). Therapists must strike a careful balance in recognizing universal couple issues and those concerns that are unique to GLB couples (Basham, 1999) to address them most effectively.

It is important to explore the effects of gender role socialization and the current expectations of each partner (Scrivner & Eldridge, 1995). Continuing to assess the development of LGB identity and its intersection with ethnicity/cultural, religious, or professional identity development (Scrivner & Eldridge, 1995) remains a critical clinical piece. Also, discovering who participates in the couple's relationship and the degree of support or interference (Patterson, Ciabattari, & Schwartz, 1999) will help guide the therapeutic process.

Rather than recognizing how the undeniable stressors over the life span impact the same-sex relationship, therapists often see the couple's repetition of struggles as ineffective or springing from personal deficits, failed development, or faulty coping skills (Slater, 1995). Couples can experience conflict in their attempt to shape their relationship and to demonstrate the seriousness of their commitment; they "invent some 'marital' rules, borrow others, and pick some to avoid as they bargain over issues that married people take for granted" (Patterson & Schwartz, 1994, p. 4).

Often it is not clear what the relationship "should" look like, even to the couple (Patterson & Schwartz, 1994). As therapists we must discern how much of the presenting problem stems from societal oppression and internalized homophobia versus normal and universal couple dynamics. Through the discovery of the contextual pieces of individual, couple, and generational stages, culture and ethnic variables, and the couple's negotiation and mobilization of family, friend, and community support, we have an increased chance of recognizing and understanding the broader and deeper clinical issues affecting same-sex couples.

REFERENCES

Barón, A., & Cramer, D. W. (2000). Potential counseling concerns of aging lesbian, gay, and bisexual clients. In R. M. Perez, K. A. DeBord, & K. J. Bieschke (Eds.), *Handbook of counseling and psychotherapy with lesbian, gay, and bisexual clients* (pp. 207-223). Washington, DC: American Psychological Association.

Basham, K. K. (1999). Therapy with a lesbian couple: The art of balancing lenses. In J. Laird (Ed.), *Lesbians and lesbian families: Reflections on theory and practice* (pp. 143-177). New York: Columbia University Press.

Bigner, J. J. (2000). Gay and lesbian families. In W. C. Nichols, M. S. Pace-Nichols, D. S. Becvar, & A. Y. Napier (Eds.), *Handbook of family development and intervention* (pp. 279-298). New York: John Wiley & Sons.

Brown, L. S. (1988). Lesbians, gay men and their families: Common clinical issues. *Journal of Gay & Lesbian Psychotherapy, 1* (1), 65-77.

Brown, L. S. (1995). Therapy with same-sex couples: An introduction. In N. S. Jacobson & A. S. Gurman (Eds.), *Clinical handbook of couple therapy* (pp. 274-291). New York: Guilford Press.

Cabaj, R. P., & Klinger, R. L. (1996). Psychotherapeutic interventions with lesbian and gay couples. In R. P. Cabaj & T. S. Stein (Eds.), *Textbook of homosexuality and mental health* (pp. 485-501). Washington, DC: American Psychiatric Press.

Davison, G. C. (2001). Conceptual and ethical issues in therapy for the psychological problems of gay men, lesbians, and bisexuals. *Journal of Clinical Psychology, 57* (5), 695-704.

Dworkin, S. (2000). Individual therapy with lesbian, gay, and bisexual clients. In R. M. Perez, K. A. DeBord, & K. J. Bieschke (Eds.), *Handbook of counseling and psychotherapy with lesbian, gay, and bisexual clients* (pp. 157-181). Washington, DC: American Psychological Association.

Falco, K. L. (1996). Psychotherapy with women who love women. In R. P. Cabaj & T. S. Stein (Eds.), *Textbook of homosexuality and mental health* (pp. 397-412). Washington, DC: American Psychiatric Press.

Goldenberg, H., & Goldenberg, I. (1998). Counseling gay male and lesbian couples. In *Counseling today's families* (3rd ed.). Pacific Grove, CA: Brooks/Cole.

Granvold, D. K., & Martin, J. I. (1999). Family therapy with gay and lesbian clients. In C. Franklin & C. Jordan (Eds.), *Family practice: Brief systems methods for social work* (pp. 299-320). Pacific Grove, CA: Brooks/Cole.

Johnson, T. W., & Colucci, P. (1999). Lesbians, gay men, and the family cycle. In B. Carter & M. McGoldrick (Eds.), *The expanded family life cycle: Individual, family, and social perspectives* (3rd ed.), pp. 346-372. Boston: Allyn & Bacon.

Matthews, C. R., & Lease, S. H. (2000). Focus on lesbian, gay, and bisexual families. In R. M. Perez, K. A. DeBord, & K. J. Bieschke (Eds.), *Handbook of counseling and psychotherapy with lesbian, gay, and bisexual clients* (pp. 249-273). Washington, DC: American Psychological Association.

Mattison, A. M., & McWhirter, D. P. (1987, Summer). Male couples: The beginning years. *Journal of Social Work and Human Sexuality, 5* (2), 67-78.

McGoldrick, M. (1989). The joining of families through marriage: The new couple. In B. Carter and M. McGoldrick (Eds.), *The changing family life cycle: A framework for family therapy* (2nd Ed.), pp. 209-233. Boston: Allyn & Bacon.

McWhirter, D. P., & Mattison, A. M. (1996). Male couples. In R. P. Cabaj & T. S. Stein (Eds.), *Textbook of homosexuality and mental health* (pp. 319-337). Washington, DC: American Psychiatric Press.

Ossana, S. M. (2000). Relationship and couples counseling. In R. M. Perez, K. A. DeBord, & K. J. Bieschke (Eds.), *Handbook of counseling and psychotherapy with lesbian, gay, and bisexual clients* (pp. 275-302). Washington, DC: American Psychological Association.

Patterson, D. G., & Schwartz, P. (1994). The social construction of conflict in intimate same-sex couples. In D. D. Cahn (Ed.), *Conflict in personal relationships* (pp. 3-26). Hillsdale, NJ: Lawrence Erlbaum.

Patterson, D. G., Ciabattari, T., & Schwartz, P. (1999). The constraints of innovation: Commitment and stability among same-sex couples. In J. M. Adams & W. H. Jones (Eds.), *Handbook of interpersonal commitment and relationship stability*. New York: Kluwer Academic/Plenum Publishers.

Reynolds, A. L., & Hanjorgiris, W. F. (2000). Coming out: Lesbian, gay, and bisexual identity development. In R. M. Perez, K. A. DeBord, & K. J. Bieschke (Eds.), *Handbook of counseling and psychotherapy with lesbian, gay, and bisexual clients* (pp. 35-55). Washington, DC: American Psychological Association.

Roth, S. (1985). Psychotherapy with lesbian couples: Individual issues, female socialization, and the social context. *Journal of Marital and Family Therapy 11* (3), 273-286.

Schiemann, J., & Smith, W. L. (1996). The homosexual couple. In H. Kessler & I. D. Yalom (Eds.), *Treating couples*. San Francisco: Jossey-Bass.

Scrivner, R., & Eldridge, N. S. (1995). Lesbian and gay family psychology. In R. H. Mikesell, D. Lusterman, & S. H. McDaniel (Eds.), *Integrating family therapy: Handbook of family psychology and systems theory* (pp. 327-344). Washington, DC: American Psychological Association.

Shernoff, M. J. (1995). Family therapy for lesbian and gay clients. In F. J. Turner (Ed.), *Differential diagnosis and treatment in social work* (pp. 911-918). New York: The Free Press.

Simons, S. (1991). Couple therapy with lesbians. In D. Hooper & W. Dryden (Eds.), *Couple therapy: A handbook* (pp. 207-216). Philadelphia: Open University Press.

Slater, S. (1995). *The lesbian family life cycle*. New York: The Free Press.

Slater, S., & Mencher, J. (1991). The lesbian family life cycle: A contextual approach. *American J. of Orthopsychiatry. 61* (3), 372-382.

Young, M. E., & Long, L. L. (1998). *Counseling and therapy for couples*. Pacific Grove: Brooks/Cole.

Clinical Issues with Gay Male Couples

Gil Tunnell
David E. Greenan

SUMMARY. Although gay male couples share with all couples three essential tasks of couplehood–creating boundaries in order to form a couple identity, negotiating closeness and distance, and accommodating to their individual differences–gay male couples face special complications in each task. These complications, examined herein, are largely the result of the marginalization gay men experience from living in a homophobic culture, and male gender acculturation that makes male-to-male intimacy difficult. A model of brief couple therapy for gay men is presented that is designed to honor, as well as challenge, the relationship the men have co-constructed and specifically addresses the difficulties men have in maintaining intimate bonds. A case study illustrates the treatment of clinical issues presented by male couples. *[Article copies available for a fee from The Haworth Document Delivery Service: 1-800-HAWORTH. E-mail address: <docdelivery@haworthpress.com> Website: <http://www.Haworth Press.com> © 2004 by The Haworth Press, Inc. All rights reserved.]*

KEYWORDS. Gay male couples, same-sex couples, male homosexuality, homophobia, gender acculturation, gay identity formation, marginalization, short-term couple therapy

---

Gil Tunnell, PhD, Private Practice, New York, NY.
David E. Greenan, EdD, The Minuchin Center for the Family, New York, NY.

[Haworth co-indexing entry note]: "Clinical Issues with Gay Male Couples." Tunnell, Gil, and David E. Greenan. Co-published simultaneously in *Journal of Couple & Relationship Therapy* (The Haworth Press) Vol. 3, No. 2/3, 2004, pp. 13-26; and: *Relationship Therapy with Same-Sex Couples* (ed: Jerry J. Bigner, and Joseph L. Wetchler) The Haworth Press, Inc., 2004, pp. 13-26. Single or multiple copies of this article are available for a fee from The Haworth Document Delivery Service [1-800-HAWORTH, 9:00 a.m. - 5:00 p.m. (EST). E-mail address: docdelivery@haworthpress.com].

http://www.haworthpress.com/web/JCRT
Digital Object Identifier: 10.1300/J398v03n02_03

13

Gay male couples are no different from all couples in needing to accomplish three basic tasks: (a) to put boundaries around their relationship that create an identity they and others respect, (b) to develop effective ways of regulating interpersonal closeness and distance within the relationship, and (c) to accommodate to their individual differences. However, the challenges that gay men experience as they take up these three tasks set them distinctly apart from opposite-sex couples (and lesbian couples). The unique functioning of the gay male couple can be attributed primarily to the fact that it is *two men* attempting to form a long-term emotional and sexual bond, a bond that violates some of society's strongest prohibitions about male gender-role behavior, as well as homosexuality. Clinical work with male couples can be challenging to therapists, yet there is also the reward of facilitating and witnessing the innovative ways in which gay men are able to create intimate relationships not based upon traditional male stereotypes (Nimmons, 2002).

The lives of couples are always embedded within the societal context of the larger culture. With gay male couples, three contextual variables–in addition to the interpersonal dynamics the couple has co-constructed–exert a centrifugal force on the men's attempt to maintain an intimate relationship: (a) the majority culture's lack of both civil and legal recognition of same-sex relationships, (b) the lack of role models and support within the gay community for the stabilization of gay unions, and (c) male gender acculturation that works against men forming intimate emotional relationships with other men.

After examining the ways that male couples differ from heterosexual couples, we describe a brief model of couple treatment designed specifically for gay men (Greenan & Tunnell, 2003), and conclude with a case study.

DISTINCTIVE CHARACTERISTICS OF MALE COUPLES

Making Boundaries

Establishing a boundary is the first task a couple faces in order to protect them from interference from other systems (Nichols & Minuchin, 1999). Boundaries, in differentiating social systems from one another, are also essential for the development of each system's identity. The identity for a couple, as a two-person system, is actively created by the two individuals, as well as bestowed on the couple by persons external to it. In this interactive process between the couple and its social context, a couple's identity is either formed and fortified, or blurred and weakened.

To forge an identity, a couple needs a supportive community. Gay couples are, by and large, denied the same level of social support accorded heterosexual married couples. When married heterosexuals present themselves socially, the couple rarely worries about having its identity acknowledged, since the culture routinely authenticates through various rituals their coupled status. For same-sex couples, homophobia causes this simple process of social validation to go awry. Because of the culture's homophobia, which the couple itself has internalized to some degree, a same-sex couple may be reticent to present itself as a "couple" to the outside world. Some coupled gay men keep their relational status invisible for years. Staying in the closet, however, is more difficult for a male couple than for a single gay man because of the heavy strain invisibility puts on the relationship. In regular dealings with society, gay couples are challenged whether to reveal their coupled status, e.g., negotiating leases, purchasing a home or major household items, sitting with the partner's family at a wedding or a funeral.

When two men come out as a couple, as increasing numbers of same-sex couples have done in the last two decades, validation by the external culture (both the mainstream culture as well as the gay subculture) is not automatically conferred. Even if the larger communities accept the gay couple's relationship as valid per se, they almost always grant it an inferior status compared to that given opposite-sex relationships (Greenan & Tunnell, 2003). That is, although now more visible within the gay community and the mainstream culture, gay male couples remain extremely marginalized. Along with interracial couples, perhaps no other type of couple faces as much discrimination from society at large. This lack of full social recognition interferes with boundary making for the couple, and adds to the couple's own experience of "relational ambiguity" (Green & Mitchell, 2002).

The gay community itself participates in the marginalization of same-sex couples. Few rituals in the gay subculture acknowledge the developmental milestone of making a long-term commitment to another man. The fluidity of same-sex relationships adds to the couple's feeling of ambiguity, as the sanctity of the male couple's relationship is frequently not respected by other gay men.

Complications in boundary making and identity formation for gay male couples are not caused simply by the culture's disallowing full social, legal or economic recognition. Gay couples often create their own relational ambiguity by challenging one or more of the traditional parameters of couplehood. Beyond the most obvious challenge to the idea that a couple must consist of a man and a woman, many male couples do not use sexual exclusivity as a way to create boundaries (Johnson & Keren, 1996). Additionally, male couples may not pool incomes or jointly own assets until many years into the relationship, if ever. Some long-term male couples never reside together. Such differences in how male couples structure their relationships are sometimes deliberate, in that male couples often develop novel relational scripts that emphasize individual autonomy. Gay men know the culture's traditional roles don't quite fit them (Kooden, 2000), and so they actively experiment with new social structures that make more sense to them.

There is yet another factor at work in why some gay couples don't conform to traditional notions of coupling. In growing up, most gay males before they actively develop a gay identity, which may not occur until young adulthood, have had to "pass" as heterosexuals to avoid social ostracism and to maintain attachment ties to significant others (Greenan & Tunnell, 2003). While necessary for social survival, the consequences of passing exact a heavy psychological toll: feeling disconnected from others, invisible, and excluded from full participation in the mainstream culture. Coming out for the gay person is an act of emancipation and the first step of true differentiation (Bowen, 1978), an expression of core individuality that risks losing connection with significant others, but without it makes an authentic connection with significant others meaningless. While coming out reduces invisibility, coming out also creates a new version of the same problem, being marginalized. Yet in being openly gay and no longer in hiding, the individual gains a spirit of autonomy. This sense of individual autonomy is often preserved in the ways gay men structure their coupled relationships. For them, relational ambiguity is not altogether negative; these gay men seem to experience a certain freedom in keeping the relationship not so defined and an enjoyment in asserting their nonconformity to cultural norms.

Family therapists may question how male couples have structured their relationships in culturally non-conforming ways. Where some couples see "freedom" in their relational ambiguity, family therapists may see instead the ways gay men are "hedging" on making fuller commitments to one another, or are colluding with the culture's marginalization of same-sex relationships. Especially in working with stigmatized minority populations who fear judgment by traditional therapists, it is critical that the therapist not insist the men fit a particular definition of a couple. On the other hand, it is easy for a therapist to "get tied up in chains" (Greenan & Tunnell, 2003), in an attempt to be politically correct or being unduly sensitive to the difficulties gay men face, and not challenge gay men to become more connected in their relationships. It *is* the therapist's job to inquire respectfully about how the couple has constructed their relationship, and to help them sort out the extent to which their boundaries and relationship structure have been purposely chosen by them, or have been created unwittingly by the culture's marginalization of them and by their own internalized homophobia. Choosing a non-traditional path in being a couple—as in being an individual—requires more, rather than less, self-examination, soul-searching, and clarification of wants and needs. A couple therapist can be the catalyst for such a dialog.

In treating male couples, the devaluing that occurs in gay men's relationships can be easily overlooked. As therapists, we have sometimes felt that we were taking the relationship more seriously than the men did. We believe, for example, it can be therapeutic to express surprise and sadness upon hearing that a couple observant of Christian traditions and together for 10 years has never spent a Christmas Day together, each joining his respective family of origin instead. While such a pattern of behavior may maintain family ties, its cost is that the couple's relationship continues to be invisible or marginalized, its boundaries remain blurred, and its identity never receives full respect.

Regulating Closeness and Distance

All couples must develop, over time, ways to regulate interpersonal distance and closeness. Some individuals enter a coupled relationship erroneously expecting the same degree of individual autonomy–behavioral as well as emotional–they enjoyed as single persons. Problems begin when one partner wants more "together time" and greater emotional connection. At the other extreme are individuals who expect to surrender almost all individual autonomy for the sake of the relationship (with the goal of "two people becoming one") and are upset when their partners are not willing to make the sacrifice. Being stuck in such an extreme complementarity–one person persistently seeking distance and other clamoring for closeness–is a recipe for misery and a major reason couples seek therapy. Truly intimate relationships require a balance of individual autonomy and interpersonal connection (Minuchin, Lee & Simon, 1996; Schnarch, 1997), although achieving this balance can take years of negotiation.

Complicating the struggle for a balance of closeness and distance is the difference in how the two genders are socialized. According to gender role theory (Gilligan, 1982; Chodorow, 1978), males in Western culture are socialized to be independent, and over time males become far more comfortable with autonomy than with emotional connection. Females are culturally conditioned to be more empathic and sensitive to others, and grow up more comfortable with relatedness than with individual autonomy. In many heterosexual couples we see in treatment, it is indeed the man who more often voices the need for distance and separation, with the woman voicing the need for emotional relatedness.[1]

Whatever difficulty straight men may have in expressing feelings, being vulnerable, and maintaining emotional connection with women, a male-female relationship is one culturally sanctioned context where such behaviors are more permissible without violating gender-role expectancies. For all men, straight or gay, it may be easier to reveal their self-doubts, admit "weakness," or express tenderness with a woman than with another man. Western culture seems to forbid overt male-to-male intimacy, sexual or emotional.

Gay men are subject to the same cultural conditioning, and indeed, may be even more sensitive about exhibiting emotional vulnerability to other men. Many gay males report shaming experiences from being taunted as youngsters by male peers and their own fathers when they displayed emotional sensitivity or exhibited other non-conforming gender role behavior, one of the early signs of a homosexual orientation (Green, 1987). To cope, most gay youth develop a "false self," managing their impressions on others to pass as heterosexual and appear as masculine as possible to stay above suspicion. The initial discovery that one is homosexual can be traumatic, not so much because the individual is discomforted by his discovery–indeed, he may find his attraction to same-sex individuals perfectly natural–but because he experiences or imagines ruptures in his attachment to significant others (Greenan & Tunnell, 2003). No one is usually there to offer steady support or guidance to the gay boy during this critical developmental phase. Indeed, parents often abandon or condemn the gay child at the very moment he most needs emotional reassurance. Although the creation of the false self allows the gay boy to maintain some degree of attachment and connectedness to others, a distancing between self and other–especially from other males–gets set up at this point and contributes later to a gay male's isolation and separateness. For many gay males, emotional autonomy becomes overdeveloped and overvalued. Later, in developing adult same-sex romantic relationships, many gay men we see in our practices find being emotionally intimate with other men inherently frightening for fear of being shamed again or, in effect, re-traumatized.

Since gay males are subject to the same cultural conditioning that all males receive, should gay male couples generally be more disengaged, as Krestan and Bepko (1980) predicted in applying gender role theory to same-sex couples? Our own clinical experiences, as well as research by Green, Bettinger and Zacks (1996), have demonstrated that it is not that simple. While some male couples are disengaged and others are enmeshed, it is in our experience more common to find a pursuer/distancer complementarity, just as in many heterosexual couples. However, the dynamics for male couples are much more complex, since the man who voices the need for connectedness may re-experience shame about his desire for emotional closeness *with a man* (Greenan & Tunnell, 2003). Not only can gay men feel shame about their desire for closeness with a man, they have well honed their skills in being emotionally self-reliant and not being dependent on other males. Furthermore, during adolescence while straight males are getting practice in heterosexual romantic relationships, gay teenagers have almost no opportunities to experiment openly with same-sex romantic relationships. For them, adolescence can be a time of intense loneliness (Savin-Williams, 1998). By the time they reach adulthood, "intimacy with another man can provoke a man to feel unmasculine and worthless, whereas distance may render him lonely and depressed. For such men, sexual orientation is experienced as a perpetual double bind, permitting no comfortable solution and causing havoc in their couple relationships" (Johnson & Keren, 1996, p. 244).

In short, many gay men bring into their coupled relationships with other men some expectation that their male partner will criticize, judge or shame him when he reveals his feelings (Greenan & Tunnell, 2003; Siegel & Walker, 1996), and thus the couple becomes over time disengaged. In contrast, other couples present for treatment with enmeshment issues. Gay men in their twenties or thirties dating for the first time often experience a desire to merge with the beloved to create and maintain the long desired closeness. Although disengagement is the more common dynamic we see with male couples, either dynamic–disengagement or enmeshment–creates stress in a relationship. Couple therapy can become an arena for each man to have novel experiences in trusting another man with his feelings, as well as developing new ways to create boundaries.

Accommodating to One Another's Differences

In all couples, the symbiotic honeymoon period eventually ends and the couple must deal with each other's differences. Once again, gender acculturation for males has taught them how to behave when in conflict with other males. Although it is a stereotype and perhaps less true in contemporary marriages, when opposite-sex couples fight, cultural conditioning supports a tendency to compromise, negotiate, and be more collaborative in resolving differences, due to the presence of a female who may bring more collaborative skills to the table, and also because of how men are taught through gender socialization to regard women as more affiliative, kinder or gentler.

Some male couples can go for months or even several years in an "enmeshed" style of engagement, based on their fantasy of what an ideal relationship should look like, i.e., symbiosis and no conflict. Sooner or later, however, individual differences emerge. In enmeshed male couples, there is a tendency to avoid open conflict as long as possible, an interim period during which the couple's dynamic can shift from enmeshment to disengagement. Indeed, many presenting complaints of male couples seeking treatment (e.g., an affair, outside sex, too much time at the office, substance abuse) can be reframed by the therapist as ways of disengaging from the partner in order to avoid open conflict through power struggles.

Once conflicts with other men can no longer be denied, men seem to have an autonomic response either to fight or flee. Far more frequently in male-male relationships than in male-female relationships, a couple will present at the first session of therapy with one or both saying, "It's over, and we need to break up." While part of that attitude is from the paucity of role models for long-term male coupled relationships, this attitude also originates in how men are socialized to resolve differences with other men: For many men, it's all about winning or losing. There can be no middle ground. Often when one man wants to end the relationship, he feels defeated, unable to dominate the other to change his thoughts, feelings or behavior. If he can't win, he's ready to admit defeat and move on.

The male gender role, into which all males–gay or straight–are indoctrinated in Western culture, exerts enormously strong restraints on male behavior. It consists of four parts: (a) "show no sissy stuff," which derives from the need for males to be different from females; (b) "be the big wheel," or the need to be superior to others; (c) "be the sturdy oak," the need to be self-reliant and independent, and (d) "give 'em hell," the need to be more powerful than others

(Brannon, 1976). None of these characteristics promotes an ability to negotiate, compromise, and collaborate. And when a man does deviate from the traditional male role, he may feel "gender role strain" (Silverstein, Auerbach, & Levant, 2002), an uncomfortable anxiety that keeps him in role.

Richard Green (1987) and Richard Isay (1989) have written about the phenomenon of the "sissy boy syndrome." As adults, gay men re-experience fears of traumatization of being labeled "sissy" or "faggot" for their same-sex erotic feelings or atypical gender behavior. These fears are, in fact, reawakened in the treatment of gay couples when the therapist challenges the men to experiment with being more vulnerable and gentler with one another as they work out their differences. The therapist may need to confront the men, e.g., "Do you have ways of talking to him so that it doesn't appear that you are hitting him with a baseball bat?" (Greenan & Tunnell, 2003). This is not to say men should not express anger at one another. But what male couples need most help with here is in developing a "middle range" of conflict-negotiation skills, rather than full-fledged fighting or fleeing the scene.

Male-male relationships are so often about power. While male-female relationships can also focus on power and control, in male couples the power dynamic is more frequently front and center, and indeed represents the flip side of the difficulty men have in maintaining emotional connection and in acknowledging dependency needs. In short, the power plays seen in gay male couples have more to do about their being male than in their being gay. The therapist must be comfortable modeling innovative ways for men to stay connected while they are in conflict, and be willing to model authenticity in communication. Couple therapy can then become a vehicle for healing old wounds of feeling estranged and cut off from others, rather than deepening the estrangement. With a sensitive and empathic therapist who is at the same time challenging, gay men learn novel ways to soothe one another and become more deeply connected. They begin to view divorce as the last option rather than the first.

CREATING A NEW WAY OF BEING: A THERAPEUTIC MODEL

As Nancy Boyd-Franklin (1989) has written about the challenges of engaging Black families in therapy, gay couples are also a marginalized minority that present for treatment with a mistrust of the majority culture. The gay couple will initially scrutinize the couple therapist to ascertain if he or she is representative of a field that has historically pathologized their sexual orientation. It is a prerequisite in working with marginalized populations that the couple therapist establish a solid therapeutic alliance as he or she joins with them and learns about their presenting problem. As the therapist explores the problems for which the couple seeks treatment, the therapist begins to forge an alliance by asking questions that communicate to the gay men respect for their relationship. Questions such as "When and how did you meet?" "What about your partner made you fall in love with him?" "What anniversary date do you celebrate?" "Do you have or are you planning to have children?" "Who honors and supports you as a couple?" communicate respect and acknowledge their couplehood. Simultaneously, the therapist uses this information to formulate hypotheses about how the men have co-constructed their relationship.

Male couples even in large urban settings can be isolated from other male couples. They may have few gay role models to normalize the stresses and transitions in the developmental life cycle of a couple. The therapeutic encounter can be an opportunity for healing as the men experience the therapist's normalization of their same-sex relationship. Additionally, it is important that the therapist communicates early in treatment the belief that they have the resources to strengthen their relationship. The therapist's expressed respect in highlighting the strengths of the relationship helps to instill within the couple feelings of hope that their relationship can be deepened. In a culture that marginalizes gay unions, this initial intervention is vital and therapeutic for the couple.

After ascertaining the couple's reasons for coming into therapy and taking a history of their relationship, the therapist is in a position, if he or she hasn't already done so, to experience the dynamics of how they have constructed a relationship that is stuck. What we find unique and therapeutic for male couples is using the *in vivo* experience of the session as an opportunity to experiment with behaviors. The therapist needs to experience the couple's behaviors that have become rigidified over time and no longer work, and then challenge the couple to experiment with new, more flexible behaviors that may prove to be more satisfying for them. Our basic tenet of treatment is that a couple has the inherent resources to solve their problems if they are provided with the necessary conditions to activate their "hidden treasures" (Genijovich, 1994). The therapist's role in treatment is to create the conditions that are conducive for the men to experiment with new ways of interacting. To do that the therapist must be comfortable with encouraging two men to reveal greater emotional vulnerability, which creates greater intimacy, and be willing to access and model his or her own inherent "feminine" qualities.

A CASE EXAMPLE

Eric and Hector came in for their initial session of couple therapy at the instigation of Hector, who told the therapist their relationship of 20 years was in jeopardy of ending due to Eric's substance abuse. It was readily apparent to the therapist that Eric was being dragged in against his better judgment. Hector, a large Dominican biracial man with a big warm smile, entered the therapist's office full of certainty and self-righteousness. He greeted the therapist with assurance and seated himself on the edge of a chair, thumping his fingers on the arm rest. Eric, his Danish American partner, slipped into the therapist's office, the sour look on his face and the way he collapsed into his chair conveying he was both discouraged and annoyed with his partner for this visit.

Hector quickly launched into a tirade about a recent vacation the couple had taken to a South American seaside resort. Eric had disappeared for the night, hanging out in a local bar until sunrise when Hector discovered him staggering back to their hotel. Hector had flown into a rage. He insisted on ending their holiday and returning to New York immediately. The therapist was able to ascertain that the drinking was behavior uncharacteristic for Eric, and both men agreed he hadn't abused alcohol or drugs since the early days of their relationship. Each of the men held responsible jobs. Eric ran a successful hedge fund, and Hector was a humanities professor in a local junior college.

By observing the enactment that had occurred at this very early stage of treatment, the therapist speculated to himself that the couple had adopted distinctly complementary roles in their relationship–the classic roles of distancer and pursuer. As the therapist observed their dynamics, the problem seemed to be the way Hector pursued and Eric's response to his partner's communication style. Hector would puff up his chest in anger. Eric responded by shrinking into his chair and turning white with rage. In a dynamic that reinforced the pattern, Eric would hunker down and retreat rather than becoming more available. Repeatedly, the couple enacted this dynamic as they tried to talk about what had happened on their holiday. The therapist assumed that the circular behavior he was observing, though by no means a complete picture of their dynamics as a couple, was characteristic of how they interacted at home. He knew he would need to share these process-level observations with Eric and Hector, but first he needed to join more with them. Although Hector appeared to be open to challenges by the therapist, Eric appeared skeptical and defensive whenever the therapist addressed him.

Being the first session, the therapist decided to explore other aspects of their relationship, to ascertain what strengths had kept them together as a couple for the past twenty years. He said that they would return to this episode that was obviously causing both of them much pain but first he would like to learn more about them as a couple. How did they meet? Had they registered as domestic partners with City Hall? Who in and outside their families supported them as a couple?

What emerged was a poignant story of two men who had first met while engaging in anonymous sex at the piers during the sexual revolution in the 1970s. Both men, though in their twenties at the time, had little or no experience socializing with and dating other gay men. For both men, gay life consisted of anonymous sex in often dangerous places. This is not an uncommon story for many young gay men even in these supposedly enlightened times where few opportunities exist for gay adolescents and young adults to meet and socialize. Bars or anonymous casual sexual environments remain for many gay men their introductory socialization to gay life.

However, Eric and Hector clicked, and both men told stories of how each would return to the piers in the hopes of once again meeting the other. Eventually they did reconnect and Eric (currently the distancer) was brave enough to ask Hector for his telephone number. Mustering up all his courage and quieting his fears of rejection, he called Hector for their first "date." Within a year after that date, they were living together. Initially the couple was isolated. It took many years for Eric to come out to his Catholic family. And to this day, Eric had never felt safe to introduce Hector to his conservative work colleagues. By day, he lived and breathed a war room culture of "kill or be killed." Hector, on the other hand, was out to his family since "birth" and felt comfortable introducing Eric to his family and coworkers. Highlighting a strength of their relationship, the therapist said he wondered if Eric's "marriage" to Hector may have been partially due to his attraction to a large warm family. For the first time in the session, both men looked at one another and smiled in agreement. The therapist then reflected to the couple that they had many strengths but, similar to other couples, they were caught in very limiting ways of interacting with one another.

Over the next few sessions, the therapist himself got stuck in a problem-solving mode of treatment and consequently the couple remained stuck. The therapist uncharacteristically stayed focused on the content of the couple's areas of conflict, i.e., could Eric be more responsible and communicate to Hector when he wanted to go out on his own so that Hector wouldn't worry? This is a fatal error in any systemic treatment as the therapist misses the process level of the couple's interactions that keeps them caught in predictable rigid behavioral patterns, i.e., Hector blowing up and Eric closing down. Furthermore, the therapist was not using his own feelings and responses to the couple to model a more empathic way of connecting.

As family therapists, we believe this use of self is particularly essential in working with gay couples because of the carefully constructed "false self" gay men have molded in their development to feel safer in a hostile, homophobic world (Greenan & Tunnell, 2003). The therapist, also a gay man, may have been responding to Hector's rage that reawakened a need to hide his essential self for fear of being shamed by another man. What this couple had not learned, and what the therapist in not using his own experience had failed to communicate, was how unsafe and bereft the sessions were in generating feelings of connectedness.

Before the next session, the therapist consulted with a senior colleague to extricate himself from the stoic, "fix it" male culture the couple had inducted him into. As he and the consultant watched the videotape of the prior session, the therapist became aware of how anxious Hector's anger made him feel. In the next session, he was able to start to use his feelings to unbalance the couple in their circular patterns of behavior. As Hector railed, the therapist gently put

his hand on Hector's arm and said, "Hector, when you puff up and start holler-
ing at Eric, I get anxious and have the desire to run away. Is your intent to scare
Eric too?" Eric peeked out of his hunkered down position. Hector paused in
his tirade. He then turned to the therapist. "No," he stammered, "but that's how
I learned to survive in a world that beats up Dominican sissies." The therapist
seeing another side of Hector for the first time said, "Have you ever told those
stories to Eric? Talk to him. He just may be available."

The therapy changed rapidly after this session as the men began to focus on
how they could be more available to one another. Tentatively, Hector began to
talk to Eric about how fearful his experience had been growing up as a boy
who was identified as "a faggot" by other boys. As the couple became more
trusting of one another, Hector was able to talk to Eric about his experiences as
a biracial man. He also revealed to Eric for the first time how traumatized he
felt from being in his classroom and watching the terrorists' attacks on 9/11. In
a later session, Hector revealed his fear of losing Eric to AIDS. Although
asymptomatic, Eric had tested sero-positive soon after the couple had met.
Like many other serodiscordant couples, over the years the men had carefully
avoided addressing the feelings of vulnerability associated with Eric's HIV
status.

In treatment they tentatively began to share their feelings of vulnerability,
tenderness and love for one another. By no stretch of the imagination did Eric
become a "touchy-feely" caretaker, but his body language and affect softened
as he listened to his crying partner. But Eric, who initially had been the identified patient in this relationship because of his distancing and disengagement,
became more available and affectionate in his own version of caretaking. In-
terestingly, as Eric listened to Hector's fears, Hector's anger diminished. Both
men gradually learned to shift and expand their roles in a more complex and
fulfilling partnership, interrupting their circular and rigid patterns of distancer
and pursuer.

The therapist was now on the right road to helping these two men discover
more intimate ways of relating. Eric began to focus on how to make the world
a safer place for his partner as Hector taught Eric how to soothe him. Simultaneously, as the men became more vulnerable and nurturing with one another,
their power struggles for control of the other gradually diminished.

CONCLUSION

The model of couple therapy described here is a relatively brief treatment,
as few as 12 sessions. Based on Salvador Minuchin's (1974) structural family
therapy, the treatment moves quickly from an initial joining stage, to observing a couple's enactments of patterned interpersonal behaviors, and finally to
unbalancing or disrupting the old circular patterns. In the initial joining stage,
the therapist must be particularly welcoming since gay men are so marginalized
by mainstream culture, often violate many culturally accepted definitions of

couplehood, and may expect judgment by mental health professionals. However, once the couple feels validated, for therapy to be effective the therapist must question and challenge the current interpersonal dynamics enacted in session that cause the couple distress. Unbalancing in this model requires a highly active therapist to set up conditions for the men to experiment with new interpersonal behaviors *in vivo*. For male couples, the new behaviors most often involve defining boundaries to forge a stronger couple identity, maintaining emotional connection while allowing individual autonomy, and learning to tolerate their individual differences without male power plays.

NOTE

1. In less polarized male-female relationships, the man may push the woman to develop more autonomy because she has not yet developed that side of herself and needs support. Likewise, many women are able to make the relationship safe enough for men to experiment with greater connectedness. Such relationships can be growth-enhancing for both individuals.

REFERENCES

Bowen, M. (1978). *Family therapy in clinical practice*. New York: Aronson.

Boyd-Franklin, N. (1989). *Black families in therapy: A multisystemic approach*. New York: Guilford Press.

Brannon, R. (1976). The male sex role: Our culture's blueprint of manhood and what it's done for us lately. In D. David & R. Brannon (Eds.), *The 49-percent majority*. Reading, MA: Addison-Wesley.

Chodorow, N. (1978). *The reproduction of mothering: Psychoanalysis and the psychology of gender*. Berkeley, CA: University of California Press.

Genijovich, E. (1994). *The impossible blended family* [Videotape]. Boston: Family Studies, Inc.

Gilligan, C. (1982). *In a different voice: Psychological theory and women's development*. Cambridge, MA: Harvard University Press.

Green, R. (1987). *The "sissy boy syndrome" and the development of homosexuality*. New Haven, CT: Yale University Press.

Green, R.-J., & Mitchell, V. (2002). Gay and lesbian couples in therapy: Homophobia, relational ambiguity, and social support. In A. S. Gurman & N. S. Jacobson (Eds.), *Clinical handbook of couple therapy* (3rd ed.). New York: Guilford Press.

Green, R.-J., Bettinger, M., & Zacks, E. (1996). Are lesbian couples fused and gay male couples disengaged? Questioning gender straightjackets. In J. Laird & R.-J. Green (Eds.), *Lesbians and gays in couples and families: A handbook for therapists*. San Francisco: Jossey-Bass.

Greenan, D. E., & Tunnell, G. (2003). *Couple therapy with gay men*. New York: Guilford Press.

Isay, R. (1989). *Being homosexual: Gay men and their development*. New York: Farrar Straus Giroux.

Johnson, T. W., & Keren, M. S. (1996). Creating and maintaining boundaries in male couples. In J. Laird & R.-J. Green (Eds.), *Lesbians and gays in couples and families: A handbook for therapists*. San Francisco: Jossey-Bass.

Kooden, H. (2000). *Golden men: The power of gay midlife*. New York: Avon Books.

Krestan, J. A., & Bepko, C. S. (1980). The problem of fusion in lesbian relationships. *Family Process, 19*, 277-289.

Minuchin, S. (1974). *Families and family therapy*. Cambridge, MA: Harvard University Press.

Minuchin, S., Lee, W.-Y., & Simon, G. (1996). *Mastering family therapy: Journeys of growth and transformation*. New York: Wiley.

Nichols, M., & Minuchin, S. (1999). Short-term structural family therapy with couples. In J. M. Donovan (Ed.), *Short-term couple therapy*. New York: Guilford Press.

Nimmons, D. (2002). *The soul beneath the skin*. New York: St. Martin's Press.

Savin-Williams, R. C. (1998). *"And then I became gay": Young men's stories*. New York: Routledge.

Schnarch, D. (1997). *Passionate marriage: Sex, love and intimacy in emotionally committed relationships*. New York: Norton.

Siegel, S., & Walker, G. (1996). Connections: Conversations between a gay therapist and a straight therapist. In J. Laird & R.-J. Green (Eds.), *Lesbians and gays in couples and families: A handbook for therapists*. San Francisco: Jossey-Bass.

Silverstein, L. B., Auerbach, C. F., & Levant, R. F. (2002). Contemporary fathers reconstructing masculinity: Clinical implications of gender role strain. *Professional Psychology: Research and Practice, 4*, 361-369.

Identity and Cultural Narrative in a Lesbian Relationship

M. Theodora Pintzuk

SUMMARY. The dynamics of a specific lesbian couple are explored in terms of identifications, identity, and cultural narratives. Problems within couples can arise from challenges to the organization of identifications and to identity within and between the individuals as a couple moves from one cultural narrative to another. Female masculinity is especially vulnerable to these transitions, as it lacks legitimization from the culture at large. *[Article copies available for a fee from The Haworth Document Delivery Service: 1-800-HAWORTH. E-mail address: <docdelivery@haworthpress.com> Website: <http://www.HaworthPress.com> © 2004 by The Haworth Press, Inc. All rights reserved.]*

KEYWORD. Lesbian couples, female masculinity, identity, identifications, cultural narrative

THE FRAME

Fantasy is an integral part of relational life, both enriching and confounding it. *Fantasy* here refers to the conscious and unconscious patterns or stories one

M. Theodora Pintzuk, LCSW, is in private practice in Chicago and is Core Faculty of the Chicago Training Collaborative: Clinical Practice with LBGT Individuals and Their Families, 3850 N. Lawndale, Chicago, IL 60618 (E-mail: jiantheo@aol.com).

[Haworth co-indexing entry note]: "Identity and Cultural Narrative in a Lesbian Relationship." Pintzuk, M. Theodora. Co-published simultaneously in *Journal of Couple & Relationship Therapy* (The Haworth Press) Vol. 3, No. 2/3, 2004, pp. 27-41; and: *Relationship Therapy with Same-Sex Couples* (ed: Jerry J. Bigner, and Joseph L. Wetchler) The Haworth Press, Inc., 2004, pp. 27-41. Single or multiple copies of this article are available for a fee from The Haworth Document Delivery Service [1-800-HAWORTH, 9:00 a.m. - 5:00 p.m. (EST). E-mail address: docdelivery@haworthpress.com].

Digital Object Identifier: 10.1300/J398v03n02_04

has regarding self, other, intimacy, sexuality, love, and the like. These are formed from the internalization of patterns in early relationships, from identifications and disidentifications with important people in one's life, and from *cultural narratives*, the adoption (and adaptation) of which is essential for becoming a cultural citizen of a particular society. Identification is the process through which one person (usually an infant or toddler) internalizes aspects of a significant other. The internalization then becomes part of that person's psychic structure. The process occurs in response to loss, usually loss on the level of imperfect maternal/paternal response, and serves as a means of maintaining connection to the absent or imperfect other. Infants are assumed to identify with both same sex and cross-sex caretakers[1] and to access these identifications equally. However, when the toddler begins to consolidate an identity as *girl* or *boy*, a *disidentification* with the cross-sex caretaker generally occurs–as the child becomes a girl, for instance, *just like mommy*. The erstwhile cross-sex identifications recede to the background; although not being really lost they can emerge if the conditions are right. For a cogent discussion of identification and disidentification, see Fuss (1995).

Cultural narratives are the more or less articulated stories or explanations developed within, and used by, cultural groups. They should not be confused with Jungian archetypes. Whereas Jung (1979) described archetypes as residing in a collective unconscious and being transhistorical in their structure and dynamics, cultural narratives are historically embedded. They express the social arrangements and values of a society, including the tensions and contestations that arise from these arrangements. They are internalized (and resisted) as part of the acculturation process of members of that society. They serve four primary functions: One is to provide meaning to the major aspects of life (e.g., what it is to be human, to be male, female, to be in a family, to come of age, to die, and so on). Secondly, cultural narratives provide general explanatory frame works that delineate the relational dynamics between groups of people within the society–especially those that have unequal power and are valued unequally. Examples of this function emerge in the explanations given justifying the relations between women and men or people of color and white people in the U.S. The third function is to naturalize the status quo, including the unequal distribution of power and resources between groups in non-egalitarian societies. An example of the naturalizing function can be seen in the extent to which same sex behavior amongst animals is ignored in research on animal behavior, while the question of heterosexuality's origins is seldom raised. Lastly, cultural narratives guide individuals as to which identifications pertain to them personally. Not entering into these narratives leaves one *illegible* (Butler, 1993), unable to make one's self understood by others.

Within the narrative of each category (white woman, black child, and so forth) are variations on the theme. I refer to these as *tropes*–figures of speech, as it were. So within the narrative of Woman/girl, there are tropes outlining the tomboy, the girly-girl, the virgin, the whore, and the mother, to name a few.

Because gender is in fact complex and various, many tropes must exist within each gender narrative for the narrative to maintain the appearance of veracity.

This paper is concerned with the relationship between identifications, identity, and cultural narratives as they interact to create subjectivity,[2] especially as this interweave shapes adult relational dynamics. It is an attempt to trace some of the intricacies of lesbian subjectivity as it is experienced in the context of a coupled relationship. Its particular focus is on a relational pattern seen within some lesbian couples in which one member of the couple foregrounds feminine identifications and the other, masculine identifications. The dynamics in this configuration are not comparable to those in heterosexual relationships, where typically body and gender coincide with cultural norms and where masculinity is legitimized.

> Gwen and Charlie (Charlotte)[3] have been with each other for 3 years. They moved in together a year after beginning to date, and mark their troubles as beginning then.
>
> The first year of their relationship was marked with healthy skirmishes in which each woman asserted her needs and limits in the context of the relationship. They were enlivened by this process, feeling compelled to be their largest selves. However, since the move, an edginess has entered into their tussles. It is this edginess and a concomitant loss of intimacy that has brought them into couples therapy.
>
> On inquiry, they "confess" to a marked diminution in their sexual lives. What had been a very passionate relationship now consists primarily of cuddling and kissing; genital contact is rare. This is less an acknowledged concern than is the loss of emotional intimacy.
>
> Despite this, they are able to communicate freely and respectfully with each other. Both are psychologically minded.

This sort of couple has been seen often enough to invite debate over the existence or not of *lesbian bed death*. The phenomenon is often explained as resulting from a relationship in which both parties have been raised to be caretakers, causing boundaries to blur and stifling healthy competitiveness; as part of the toll that external and internalized homophobia take on lesbian relationships; as the product of heterosexism, so that lesbianism and lesbian sexuality in particular are insufficiently or negatively mirrored; as arising from the damage done to female sexuality generally under patriarchy, in which sexual abuse of girls is rampant and the sexual suppression of women is *de rigueur*; as well as by the concerns typical of all couples: power struggles, issues of autonomy or its lack, poor communication, and poor problem-solving skills. All of these may in fact be playing a role in the breakdown of Gwen and Charlie's relationship. However, I am focusing elsewhere–on the vicissitudes of identity within the context of a lesbian relationship, and on the role of cultural narratives in bolstering or undermining identity.

Both Gwen and Charlie are strong personalities. They identify one of their strengths to be their ability to go toe to toe with each other, and they share a sense of finally finding someone big enough to meet and contain her. Initially, they experienced the push and pull as exhilarating. It called on each to be her best self. But over the last year or more, power struggles have increasingly replaced the mutual demand to be fully present to each other. At first they accepted their disappointment at this, assuming it to be a part of settling into a long-term relationship. Then they began to worry about their future together, which brought them into therapy.

Perhaps the initial "call and response" of the first year arose from more than the to-be-expected idealizing bliss of the honeymoon stage. In lesbian relationships, idealization may also be a reaction formation defense against the shaming of homophobia (and sexism). In order for her to love *as a lesbian*, she must either protect herself from homophobia's corrosive effects to her lesbian identity or metabolize her internalized homophobia, a process that may take decades. Idealization of lesbians, women, outlaw sexuality, or queerness often serves as a buffer from homophobia's toxicity. However, the vicissitudes of daily life tend to erode idealization, leaving the woman more exposed, thus tainting her sense of lesbianism. This may make transitions within lesbian relationships fraught, especially when combined with the common belief that lesbian relationships don't last and are an arena for drama. In addition, the lack of available role models for lesbian relationships may help promote the fantasy that lesbian relationships are substantially different than heterosexual ones, that they are supposedly a break from life as lived in a heterosexual nuclear family.

Gwen is the oldest of 3 girls, born of parents who arrived in the U.S. from Italy as children. Her father did his best to enforce patriarchal rule and custom through physically and verbally attacking his daughters when they stepped out of line regarding family obligations or indications of sexual freedom. Her mother retreated rather than protect the girls, only to emerge when he was absent. Then she would be full of a sort of over-blown festivity, expressed through shopping sprees, elaborate meal preparation, and card parties with her "girlfriends."

Charlie, on the other hand, came from a family emotionally ruled by her mother. Her mother loved and hated largely, and expressed that not only within the family but also within a close-knit circle of women friends. Whatever she did, she did in grand terms, throwing herself fully into it and making claims for her way of doing things as the best, sanest, most life-giving way. Charlie's father, the calming pole of the marriage, often receded into the shadows cast by the mother's flames. His work and hobbies were almost always backgrounded.

Lesbians, like everyone else, have internalized the patterns of early attachments (Stern, 1985) and transfer those patterns (with their concomitant styles of relating, assumptions, and expectations) onto later relationships. Perhaps both have transferred onto the other an expectation of the other's inconsistency and capacity to disappoint or outright abandon, or to overwhelm; certainly both have had small tastes of their worst fears at the hands of the other.

Perhaps the troubles in their relationship arise in part from their having moved into a more defended mode to avoid retraumatization. However, while understanding the role of early genetic material in shaping current romantic relationships is important, an understanding of lesbian dynamics has to include recognition of dynamics particular to lesbian relationships.

The dynamics that shape emotional and sexual intimacy amongst lesbians have been addressed by roughly two camps of thought. One group, strongly identified with the women's liberation and lesbian liberation movements, has emphasized the effects of homophobia as a cultural phenomenon and of sex role socialization in a same sex pair on challenges to, and strengths of, the lesbian couple (Boston Lesbian Psychologies Collective, 1987; Burch, 1993, 1997; Falco, 1991; Garnets & Kimmel, 1993; Glassgold & Iasenza, 1995; Laird, 1999; Loulan, 1987; Slater, 1995). The emphasis in this groundbreaking work has been on the cultural shaping of lesbian relationships, especially through sex role socialization, oppression, stigma management, and inadequate mirroring. Lesbians are seen as historically located and socially constructed, but the complexity of subjectivity within the matrix of acculturation and resistance is downplayed. Lesbian subjectivity–and the role of gendering in the creation of subjectivity–is not treated in a coherent manner.

A second tradition, more closely aligned with feminist and queer psychoanalysis, focuses more on the development of subjectivity through identifications, desire, gender and sexuality, from pre-lesbian infancy and childhood through lesbian adulthood (Butler, 1993; Dimen, 1996, 2000; Elise, 1998, 2000; Fast, 1999; Harris, 1996, 2000, 2003; Schwartz, 1998). While attending to these subtle and complex issues, these writers tend to let slip from their view how subjectivity plays out within couples outside the therapeutic dyad, as well as the effects on subjectivity of stigma management.

Drawing from both bodies of literature, I am attending to the interaction of three force fields, as it were, active in the creation and shaping of subjectivity. They are the intrapsychic processes of identification and disidentification, the process of identity development that is both intrapsychic and interpersonal/socially, and the parameters set by cultural narratives on both these processes. That lesbians have a "spoiled identity" (Goffman, 1963) and lead (to the sensibility of the dominant culture) "illegible" lives highlight the importance of cultural narratives in the development of subjectivity.[4]

THE HEART OF THE MATTER

Retuning to Gwen and Charlie, it is possible to trace (albeit in crude form) the interaction of identifications and identity within each woman, and then to show how they influence the shaping of relational dynamics. It can be assumed that each began life with primary identifications with their mothers, who were both their primary caretakers and same-sex parents (Chodorow, 1978). As they learned themselves to be girls, and subsequently as they learned and created meanings for that category, their maternal identifications became modified, more complex, and mixed with cross-identifications.

Charlie identified with her mother's "larger than life" style. This identification was particularly useful as she became a tomboy;[5] she used ferocity to face the taunting she got at school for "thinking she was a boy." Yet, in her family, ferocity was seen as a female characteristic, and Charlie identified as masculine from an early age. To make use of her mother's ferocity, Charlie had to recast it in masculine form so as to keep her masculine identity stable.

She became aware of being attracted to girls early, by age 7. While she had crushes on other schoolgirls, the primary object of her great girlhood courtship (felt with all the ferocity of her tomboy self) was of her mother. That she was conscious of her attraction to girls and that her thinking was at an operational level combined to underscore her interest in (re)claiming male identifications, as she understood gender as something literal and concrete, needing to be in line with her attractions. Also, her body had "betrayed" her–she was taller and larger than girls were "supposed" to be in her culture, and she managed that misfit by reading masculinity into it. She came into puberty with a sense of a gap between both her masculine and feminine identifications on the one hand and what she knew herself to be on the other hand. That is, where she was like her mother, she failed at being truly female; where she was like her father, she failed at being actually male. To ward off the confusion and shame of being so deficited and Illegible as a cultural citizen, Charlie worked hard during adolescence to develop an identity as a romantic gentleman, a softhearted and self-sacrificing masculinity (not unlike her father, but with the boldness of her mother). In her early twenties she channeled her tomboy-ness into karate training and through that developed a second masculine narrative for herself–that of warrior. By the time she entered into the relationship with Gwen, she had two decades of experiences focusing on the beloved, maintaining the beloved on a pedestal, and serving/sacrificing herself for the other from a masculine position. Like her mother, she made relationships–romantic relationships and friendships–her primary focus; like her father, she tended not to place her own ambitions and needs in the limelight. True to her tomboy self, she resisted the inevitable loss of freedom to adult responsibility; after all, how does a tomboy become a man?

When Charlie entered my consulting room, she was a complex blend of feminine and masculine identifications with a well-developed masculine identity. This identity allowed her to give a masculine cast to what might otherwise be seen as feminine roles and positions within relationships, saving her from facing her sense of inferiority as a woman or her fear of vulnerability.[6]

> Gwen, assertive and adventuresome as a girl, never felt the need to take on a masculine identity. Her heroes were Wonder Woman and Batwoman. She also didn't experience herself as attracted to girls/ women until her sophomore year of college. Until then, her romantic and sexual interest centered around boys. Thus she had no need to develop a sexual narrative of herself from a masculine position. Nonetheless, she also came out of adolescence with a complex interplay of feminine and masculine identifications, this time organized by a feminine identity.
>
> As she moved into adolescence, Gwen sought a feminine sexuality that could blend being luscious with being bold and assertive, a sexuality of power that did not abdicate the position of the beloved. Such a sexuality both fit with her personality and was designed to protect her against following in her mother's footsteps, in terms of sexual relationships. Gwen's own experience of domination by her father, her witnessing the domination of her mother, and her identification with her mother all motivated her to create a sexual identity which would guarantee she was the "queen bee" rather than be vulnerable to being controlled by another's sense of entitlement. In this way, she was secretly borrowing her father's position as "cock of the roost." Thus was her feminine identity interwoven with masculine identifications.
>
> Despite her feminine identity, she felt she was a gender outsider. Her sexuality was a source of power and demanded a position of centrality. Those who didn't like her style referred to her as a "ball buster."

By the time Gwen entered my consulting room she had two decades of learning how to use sensuality and strong-mindedness to assure her position and protect her from being vulnerable to control or domination by others.

Amongst other factors, the fit between Gwen and Charlie was made of a particular layering of gendered identifications and identity. While both women used gendered identifications and cross-identifications in their articulation of self, their sexual identities[7] were organized primarily around a single gendering that were each complementary of the other. Both used gender defensively to protect against vulnerability and to enhance a sense of power; in a sense, their genders were eroticized. At the same time, gender was an arena of creativity and potential for both women. In entering into this relationship, they had to create a relationship "myth" (Pillari, 1993) that could accommodate the complexities and significance of their genderings. The myth had to allow Charlie's female masculinity laced with feminine identifications as well as Gwen's femininity steeled by foregrounded masculine identifications. It had to allow the defensive aspects of each woman's gender to remain intact (although I would argue that all relationships should eventually help the participants modify the defensive aspects of their gender identity).

The material from which a couple draws to create their myth includes family of origin myths, personal myths, and cultural narratives. For Gwen and Charlie, a mix of outsider and mainstream tropes was the most salient. The outsider tropes included "lesbian as Amazon" and "woman as central and primal force." The salient mainstream narrative was of a particular strain of romantic love–with the trope of the Queen and her Champion. And, of course, in the underbelly lay the mainstream narratives and tropes of lesbians as defective and women as lesser.

In the trope of Queen and Champion, the Queen is the central figure, adored by the Champion and ruling the "realm"; she may have to sacrifice her yearnings for dependency for the sake of sovereignty. She loves the Champion's boldness and adventure. Her love inspires and strengthens the Champion to face ordeals, sacrifices, and risks in the Queen's service, in order to prove worthy of the love which fuels her. A cycle of idealization and sacrifice powers this trope. As a neglected trope of Romantic love, and as one featuring the centrality of Woman, the Queen/Champion trope served Gwen's and Charlie's purposes well. It left the gendered organization intact (dominant femininity with a masculinity that serves/services) while bolstering and romanticizing their shared sense of outsider-ness.

> Gwen was most certainly a queen. She was unequivocal about the attention and respect due her, as well as generous with her attentions and ministrations. She saw herself as a power to be contended with, and demanded the same of her lovers. Charlie gladly met the challenge. Gwen led with the unspoken demand that her powerful partner attend to her, which, when softened, turned into yearnings to be taken care of.
>
> Charlie had demands of Gwen as well. Gwen had to be powerful, even in her vulnerability. She had to be able to stand up to Charlie's idealization of her. She had to be able to meet Charlie's large energy without flinching (this allowed Charlie to experience herself as large and powerful). And she had to admire Charlie for her adventures and sacrifices of self.

The cultural narrative served as an organizer of transferences,[8] both augmenting and undermining those arising from intrapsychic dynamics. In the same way that intrapsychic transference have a leading and trailing edge (Tolpin, 2002), so does the cultural narrative's influence on the transference.

Speaking from the perspective of cultural studies, Munt (1991) describes the common practice amongst lesbians of developing proud lesbian identity as a defense against, rather than resolution of, internalized homophobia. Although she is not using the language of psychoanalysis, she is identifying a leading and trailing edge phenomenon. The dynamics of the Queen/Champion narrative, with its lionizing of women and the encouragement for idealization, served as a counter to the disrespect and maltreatment both experienced as women and lesbians. In addition, for Charlie as a gender-variant person, the leading edge of the narrative of Champion/Warrior created the potential for her to have an embodied[9] pride in self. However, insofar as the narrative provided only the *illusion* of being superior to the vicissitudes of stigmatized identities, the women were required to continually keep at bay the shame generated by their spoiled identities. Challenges to the integrity of the Queen/Champion trope undermined its capacity to contain and keep shame at bay.

> Once they moved in together, Gwen expected Charlie to take more responsibility for "maintaining the realm." Charlie rose to the occasion, reducing the time she spent at karate training and with friends; instead, she threw herself into her work in a way that won her promotions. As training and being with friends faded and work became more central to her life, she took pride in her sense of developing adulthood. By casting this new phase of her life as a "real life test" of her warriorship, she was better able to cope with missing her old life and the resentment she felt toward Gwen for having to give it up.
>
> During this time, tension between the two women grew as Charlie felt overtaxed and Gwen felt unsupported and uncared for–this as Charlie focused less on Gwen and more on her work. It was in this period that their sex life began to falter.

The breakdown was, in a sense, the result of Gwen–with Charlie's consent–trying to move Charlie from Champion to King. The King shares governance with the Queen and is equally concerned with the welfare of the realm and the accumulation of power and mastery. Charlie felt that this was her ultimate challenge, the ordeal that would certainly prove herself worthy of Gwen. And, in fact, Gwen was calling her to move forward into adulthood from what had been a stalled developmental process, stalled because of the dilemmas presented Charlie by her gender variance. She struggled in making this transition. It required her to create an adult/mature construct of female masculinity when there existed no cultural narrative or trope to support such. Insofar as her masculinity served defensive functions, protecting her from feelings of shame and powerlessness, any modification of her masculine identity had to proceed cautiously. Insofar as it served as a fundamental organizer of the psyche,[10] again, caution was called for. Charlie was cathected to the position of Champion, felt most embodied and most powerful there. As Champion, Charlie was functioning from a position of power, which could then be gifted to Gwen. She felt no libidinal charge[11] to King, and the more she moved into that position, the less access she had to her sexuality. Her masculinity did not have enough sense of authority and agency to it to allow her to feel powerful as the King. As she strained to take on King, she was confronted with her sense of the illegitimacy of her masculinity. This conflux created a gravitational pull against Charlie easily moving into a King position.

At the same time, Gwen's organization around the trope of Queen was being destabilized. She felt pulled out of Queen and into Mother by Charlie's inability to take charge as an adult. She resented the loss of power and the relative vulnerability in this new position, and felt desexualized by it. It also brought her identification with her own mother too much to the forefront for her comfort (Schwartz, 1998). Concurrently, Charlie's ability to meet her intensity and to match her proclivity for living a little larger than life enabled Gwen to experience containment of her energy and grandiosity. All of this stirred up in Gwen her backgrounded wish to be taken care of. But to allow this to happen with Charlie in the position of Champion, Gwen would have to become something like a damsel in distress, which resonated too much against her experiences of victimhood. Instead of opening to these various forms of vulnerability, she pressured Charlie to "grow up" and be King. But that was an unsatisfactory solution, as Gwen was then threatened with losing the centrality of her position of "beloved" as Charlie became a co-administrator rather than a lover. Thus the balance of power was tilting as the defensive aspects of their identities faltered.

Identity has a private and public face to it. The private face is concerned with the organization of identifications into a narrative that is reasonably cohesive. The public face is concerned with the organization of interpersonal meanings. Oftentimes for lesbians, the private face–the organization of identifications into a narrative–doesn't find an easy match with the available cultural narratives. There are no positively valenced cultural narratives of masculine women who boast of sexual prowess through their ability to service their partners. Nor are there positively valenced cultural narratives for feminine women who are sexually drawn to women, whether masculine or feminine. Oftentimes lesbians, as an aspect of their identity integration, are required to rework the available cultural narratives to enable them to serve peculiarly lesbian ends. However, these re-workings never have the sense of legitimacy that the mainstream narratives can claim; lesbian narratives are subject to disintegration when removed from lesbian-affirming space.

To some extent, the difficulty that Gwen and Charlie experienced in transitioning from one trope to another is the consequence of the function of cultural narratives to defensively stabilize both the psyche and interpersonal relationships. To move smoothly from one trope or narrative to another, as an aspect of identity development or as an expression of the multiple aspects of a self, requires either that a variety of relevant tropes and narratives be available or that the need for the defensive function has been modified. Otherwise, moving from one narrative or a trope to another can mean stepping into a place of illegibility and shame. An example of this can be seen in the early stages of coming out, as the woman is beginning to dispute her heterosexual identity. This is often felt as a period of illegibility, in which one is vulnerable to the shaming of being "abject" (Butler, 1993). Moving out of a viable trope when there is nothing else taking its place can invite either a loss of meaning to the self or a sudden vulnerability to the shame that the trope had staved off. For Charlie, the lack of "tom-men" created such a loss and such vulnerability. For Gwen, the difficulty of maintaining a stance in which femininity can be claimed from a position of strength was magnified by the difficulties posed her by Charlie as Champion and as King. She was constrained by the lack of cultural narratives of women as both sexual and wielding authority. The strains in their relationship were a reflection of the internal strains they both experienced as they worked on creating cultural narratives for themselves from a larger culture that saw them as fundamentally illegible.

DENOUEMENT

Through tracing the intermingling of identifications, identity, and cultural narrative in Gwen and Charlie's relationship, a means of highlighting the dynamics unique to lesbian relationships emerges. While the processes of coming together around identifications, identity building, and use of fantasy are the same for lesbian and heterosexual couples, the conditions in which these processes occur are not the same. The fit between one's self experience and narrative, and cultural narratives, influences how identifications will be foregrounded into identity, how change will be tolerated, and whether there is support for an individual's or a relationship's maturational process. The creativity and vulnerability of female masculinity, and its subsequent influence on the lesbian relationship, become more understandable.

For Charlie and Gwen to restore the vitality of their relationship, they needed to address the defensive uses to which they employed the cultural narratives with which they identified. The position of Queen provided Gwen an incomplete corrective for her experience growing up, and protected her from the anxiety that arose when Charlie strayed from adoration. In time, she was able to recognize that the Queen was polarized against a scared, emotionally neglected and shame-filled part of her much in need of care and healing. As she worked through the childhood traumas encapsulated in this part, she was less threatened by her own vulnerability, less demanding of attention and centrality, and more able to give as well as take attention. The more she opened herself to other possible organizations of her subjectivity, letting Queen be one of many, the more she came directly in touch with her masculine identifications. During this process, she had to revisit the negative views of the feminine embedded in her identifications with her father (as well as acknowledge the Queen's incorporation of her father's tyranic interpersonal style). These, along with a sense of lesbianism as "unnatural," emerged as the defensive functions of the Queen narrative softened. Her exploration of this territory provided a new crisis in the relationship with Charlie. The crisis had two aspects to it. Charlie was not ready to embrace her own female identifications in a sexualized way or to explore masculine on masculine sexuality, so that their sexual relationship experienced an awkwardness for a period. Also, Charlie had used Gwen's tight leash to deflect her from focusing on life issues central to her well being, and with Gwen less demanding, Charlie was a bit thrown adrift with herself. They weathered both crises, in part helped by their beginning to de-reify identities that had been dearly held. Given their generally level psychic cohesion, allowing identities to become more fluid made them less demanding of the other as an assistant in defensive and regulatory functions.

For Charlie, it was essential that she find a resolution to the dilemma presented her by a masculine identity within a female body in order to relax her defensive use of the Champion. She had to resolve two aspects of the dilemma. The first involved becoming more confident in her masculinity, especially as her body belied her gender. This included Charlie creatively developing a sexuality that both enlivened all of her body while maintaining a masculine sensibility. A difficult task faced by many masculine women is laying claim to, and libidinizing, their genitals and breasts without sacrificing their masculinity. The second was to develop a mature masculinity, one that allowed her to take on adult responsibilities. Both required, and allowed, her to explore other configurations of masculinity, including less phallic masculinities, and to reclaim female identifications. This led her to a difficult period of identifying with her father, the least valued member of her family. She was able to revitalize her relationship with him, and discovered a role model for masculine softness that helped her in her quest. Paradoxically, as she developed a *soft masculinity,* she became more willing to set limits and assert her own needs with Gwen. Of course, power struggles and disappointments were part of this terrain, as Gwen's relinquishing the Queen as her primary trope didn't always occur on the same timing as Charlie's movement away from the Champion.

This is a work still in progress. As Gwen and Charlie have been able each to embrace a subjectivity that has multiple identifications and identities available to it, their gendering and sexuality have become more relaxed and fluid. While Gwen will probably always retain a more feminine cast to her identity, and Charlie a more masculine cast, neither is caught in playing out in herself, or demanding in the other, a particular manifestation of gender. This can be seen in the falling away of Charlie using sex to mirror her masculinity when that needed bolstering and of Gwen using sex to bolster a sense of herself as adorable. Needless to say, the work was fraught with many periods of anxiety, pain, and fear. Often, we excitedly explored an avenue that turned out to be no more than a cul-de-sac. Always, the creativity, integrity, and courage of the two women won out.

NOTES

1. I do not mean to imply neccessarily a two-parent, heterosexual family. Without a more involved discussion of the infant's identification with a caretaker's own feminine and masculine identifications, suffice to say that regardless of family configuration, the infant has available to it males and females, feminines and masculines, environmentally if not in its immediate family.

2. I use the term *subjectivity* rather than *self* (although both point to the same phenomenon) because it leans away from reification and more toward the process of being a self and because it points outwardly as well as inwardly for the shaping of that process. A *subject* is the "locus of experience" (Flax, 1993), whose self-awareness is shaped by the cultural syntax in which she is located. Subjectivity embraces the body, but cannot experience separate from the social construction of that particular body.

3. Gwen and Charlie are both composite portraits of several clients of mine who fall into either the "Gwen" or the "Charlie" pattern. These are not the only two patterns I have seen, but space allows only for the exploration of these two and their interaction.

4. From the perspective of sociology, Goffman studied the way stigma creates what he referred to as "spoiled identities"–shed identities of less value. Butler, approaching the same phenomena from a feminist and queer philosophical perspective, explored the mutual creation of "normal" and "abject" (Goffman's stigmatized) and how the abject are so outside the cultural logic as to be unintelligible–or "illegible"–to those within the culture.

5. I am skipping over the very important discussion of how a gender identity arises, especially when it is a cross identity–taking the gender attributed to the other sex. This begging of the question is in response to how complex that process is, how little we can say for sure about it, and the likelihood that such a discussion would occupy an entire article by itself.

6. Here is an example of the power of cultural narratives. While her earliest, most immediate experience of what it means to be a woman came from her powerful mother, nonetheless, her mother was situated in a social matrix, one in which both Charlie and her mother contended with constructions of the meaning of "woman" and "female" that post inferiority and lack of entitlement. These narratives entered into their understandings of themselves, and onto their relationship as they entered into the world about them.

7. By *sexual identity* I am referring to the organization and expression of sexuality, and the aesthetics thereof.

8. The transferential dimension of cultural narratives can be seen as part of the "story line" of selfobject transferences, such as Charlie's idealization of Gwen. It can also be seen as providing a trans-historic, naturalizing quality to internalized object transferences. For instance, Gwen's wish to be taken care of is defended against by her assuming the role of Queen, who is the center of attention without having to risk dependency.

9. An *embodied* sense of self can be difficult for gender variant people, since their bodies do not symbolize their gender, as do the bodies of gender-normative people. One of the extra-developmental tasks of gender variant people is the creation of a psychic strategy for coping with the discordance between the body as felt experience and the body as symbolic of gender.

10. This is true of all gender identities, not just Charlie, or masculine women, or lesbians.

11. Libidinal energy is the psychic component of sexuality. When a person has charged a cultural narrative with libidinal energy, the narrative then serves either to organize or to galvanize sexual energy in and for that person–or both. The libidinizing of cultural narratives is an important example of how these narratives are simultaneously inside and outside the individual, private and public.

REFERENCES

Boston Lesbian Psychologies Collective (Ed.). (1987) *Lesbian psychologies: Explorations and challenges.* Urbana, IL: University of Illinois Press.

Burch, B. (1993). *On intimate terms: The psychology of difference in lesbian relationships.* Urbana, IL: University of Illinois Press.

_____(1997). *Other women: Lesbian/bisexual experience and psychoanalytic views of women.* New York: Columbia University Press.

Butler, J. (1993). *Bodies that matter: On the discursive limits of "sex."* New York: Routledge.

Chodorow, N. (1978). *The reproduction of mothering: Psychoanalysis and the sociology of gender.* Berkeley, CA: University of California Press.

Dimen, M. (1996). Bodytalk. *Gender and Psychoanalysis: An Interdisciplinary Journal, 1* (3) 385-402.

_____(2000). The body as Rorschach. *Studies in gender and sexuality:Psychoanalysis–cultural studies–treatment–research. 1* (1) 9-40.

Elise, D. (1998). Gender repertoire: Body, mind and bisexuality. *Psychoanalytic dialogues: A journal of relational perspectives.* 8 (3) 353-372.

_____(2000) Women and desire: Why women may not want to want. *Studies in gender and sexuality: Psychoanalysis–cultural studies–treatment–research.* 1 (2) 121-145.

Falco, K. L. (1991). *Psychotherapy with lesbian clients: Theory into practice.* New York: Brunner/Mazel, Inc.

Fast, I. (1999). Aspects of core gender identity. *Psychoanalytic Dialogues: A Journal of Relational Perspectives, 9* (5) 633-661.

Flax, J. (1993). *Disputed subjects: Essays on psychoanalysis, politics and philosophy.* New York and London: Routledge.

Garnets, L. D. & Kimmel, D. C. (Eds). (1993). *Psychological perspectives on lesbian and gay male experiences.* New York: Columbia University Press.

Glassgold, J. & Iasenza, S. (Eds.) (1995). *Lesbians and psychoanalysis: Revolutions in theory and practice.* New York: The Free Press.

Goffman, E. (1963). *Stigma: notes on a spoiled identity.* NJ: Prentice-Hall.

Harris, A. (1996). Animated conversation: Embodying and gendering. *Gender & psychoanalysis: An interdisciplinary journal, 1* (3), 361-383.

_____(2000a). Politicized passions: A discussion of Diane Elise's essay. *Studies in gender and sexuality: Psychoanalysis–Cultural Studies–Treatment–Research, 1* (2), 147-156.

_____(2000b). Gender as a soft assembly: Tomboy's stories. *Studies in gender and Sexuality: Psychoanalysis–Cultural Studies–Treatment–Research,* 1(3), 223-250.

Jung, C. G. (1979). *The collected works of C. G. Jung.* H. Read, M. Fordham, G. Adler, & W. McGuire, (Eds.), and R.F.C. Hull, (Trans). Princeton, NJ: Princeton University Press.

Laird, J. (Ed.) (1999). *Lesbians and lesbian families: Reflections on theory and practice.* New York: Columbia University Press.

Loulan, JoAnn (1987). *Lesbian passion: Loving ourselves and each other.* San Francisco: Spinsters/Aunt Lute.

Munt, S. R. (Ed.).(1998). *Butch/femme: Inside lesbian gender.* London: Cassell.

Pillari, V. (1993). *Family myths in therapy.* Northvale, NJ: Jason Aronson, Inc.

Schwartz, A. E. (1998). *Sexual subjects: Lesbians, gender and psychoanalysis.* New York: Routledge.

Slater, S. (1995). *The lesbian family life cycle.* New York: The Free Press.

Stern, D. N. (1985). *The interpersonal world of the infant: A view from psychoanalysis and developmental psychology.* New York: Basic Books.

Tolpin, M., MD (2002). *Psychoanalyis of normal development.* In Goldberg, A., MD (Ed.) *Progress in Self Psychology,* Vol. 18. Hillsdale, NJ: The Analytic Press.

Bisexual Issues
in Same-Sex Couple Therapy

Mary Bradford

SUMMARY. The bisexual identity of a partner in a same-sex couple may not be an issue in the relationship, or it may introduce fear, mistrust, and divisiveness. Mixed-orientation couples face problems stemming from the dichotomizing of sexuality, negative myths and stereotypes, and lack of awareness of models and resources. It can be particularly problematic when a partner's bisexuality is first addressed within a committed relationship. Case examples illuminate some of the issues. Therapeutic tasks include addressing the context of oppression, assessing developmental stages of sexual identity and the relationship, clarifying personal meanings of bisexuality, providing education and resources, and, possibly, facilitating negotiations regarding safer sex and polyamory. Optimal couple therapy provides affirmation of bisexuality, validation of same-sex relationships, and reflection of the partner's and relationship's strengths. *[Article copies available for a fee from The Haworth Document Delivery Service: 1-800-HAWORTH. E-mail address: <docdelivery@haworthpress.com> Website: <http://www.HaworthPress.com> © 2004 by The Haworth Press, Inc. All rights reserved.]*

KEYWORDS. Bisexual, couple, relationship, sexual identity, therapy

---

Mary Bradford, PhD, Private Practice, Berkeley, CA 94704.

[Haworth co-indexing entry note]: "Bisexual Issues in Same-Sex Couple Therapy." Bradford, Mary. Co-published simultaneously in *Journal of Couple & Relationship Therapy* (The Haworth Press) Vol. 3, No. 2/3, 2004, pp. 43-52; and: *Relationship Therapy with Same-Sex Couples* (ed: Jerry J. Bigner, and Joseph L. Wetchler) The Haworth Press, Inc., 2004, pp. 43-52. Single or multiple copies of this article are available for a fee from The Haworth Document Delivery Service [1-800-HAWORTH, 9:00 a.m. - 5:00 p.m. (EST). E-mail address: docdelivery@haworthpress.com].

http://www.haworthpress.com/web/JCRT
Digital Object Identifier: 10.1300/J398v03n02_05

There are many potential pressures on same-sex relationships: cultural homophobia, rejection by family members, heterosexist laws, and the resultant wounds of low self-esteem and addictive coping responses. The partners, at least, usually share a common bond of oppression and access to a supportive subculture. But when bisexuality is an additional factor, there is a potential for divisiveness, mistrust, rupture, fear, and the introduction of differences in power and privilege.

For some couples, one or both partner's bisexuality creates no conflict. It is an accepted, even celebrated part of identity and of the richness of the mix of personality factors and life experiences. But for those for whom it presents a problem, couple therapy can be a valuable means of deepening communication and furthering intimacy by aiding the exploration of meanings of sexual identity for the partners, clarifying and expressing feelings, and negotiating ways of handling differences.

BISEXUALITY IN CONTEXT

Despite the Kinsey studies (Kinsey, Pomeroy, & Martin, 1948; Kinsey, Pomeroy, Martin, & Gebhard, 1953) which revealed that sexuality exists on a continuum, and the Klein grid (Klein, Sepekoff, & Wolf, 1985) which offered a multivariant model of sexuality and depicted its flexibility and potential fluidity, we still live in a culture that dichotomizes sexual orientation and recognizes only two choices: gay or straight. Unacknowledged, bisexual people, like other bicultural people, experience pressure to choose between aspects of their identity, feel invisible in their wholeness, and are met with discrimination from the dominant culture for being "too queer" and the sexual minority subculture as "not queer enough." They are negatively stereotyped as promiscuous, untrustworthy, indecisive, cowardly, and the bearers of HIV. The lack of visible positive bisexual role models or bisexual community complicates their identity development, self-disclosure, and relationships.

It is important to note here that our ability to generalize about bisexual women and men in relationships is limited by the great diversity of the population (Rust, 1996). There are differences in experience based on biological sex, gender, age, and sexual and relational lifestyle. Women, for instance, may feel more permission to identify as bisexual, whereas the culture is less accepting of bisexual men. Young people may be more open about their bisexuality than older people. Those in polyamorous relationships face different challenges than those who are monogamous. Ethnic, racial, cultural, and religious factors all have further impact on the acceptance and expression of bisexuality. People of color (especially men) are less likely to feel free to be open about bisexuality or to have access to supportive bisexual role models.

BISEXUAL PARTNERS

Bisexual women and men have issues in common with lesbian and gay partners, such as coming out to self and others, internalized homophobia, discrimination, and physical danger. They also have distinct concerns related to the denial of validity of their bisexuality, including the pressure to conform to dichotomous thinking about sexuality, the challenge of forming and maintaining a positive identity despite its pathologization, and the absence of a supportive network of other bisexuals. In addition, their bisexual identity itself may be a source of conflict with lesbian or gay partners who are influenced by biphobia (prejudice against bisexuality) in the gay and lesbian community (Matteson, 1996; Rust, 1995) or by negative myths and stereotypes about bisexuality in the culture at large (Hutchins & Kaahumanu, 1991). For example, lesbian partners may view bisexuality as a betrayal of lesbian community and solidarity, or gay partners may see bisexuality as an immature phase of gay development. Either may think that a bisexual person cannot be trusted to commit to relationship.

A bisexual person in a same-sex relationship is often more involved in lesbian/gay community than with the straight community and may wonder, "How do I meet my needs for affiliation with other-sex people or straight community without threatening my relationship?" One may also ask, "Do I have to negate my past relationships/present attractions because of her/his insecurity or fears regarding my bisexuality?" and "Can I be fully seen, accepted, or do I need to hide part of myself?"

Disclosure

A major problem for a bisexual person in a committed relationship occurs when her or his bisexuality was not discovered, addressed, or experienced before entering the relationship. When coming out "bi" happens within the context of committed partnership, there may be confusion about the meaning of this awareness, conflicts (intrapersonal and interrelational) over the form that its exploration will take, and fear of a threat to the stability of the relationship.

LESBIAN AND GAY PARTNERS

Problems for lesbian and gay partners of bisexuals can stem from negative stereotypes and myths, from lack of understanding of the meaning of bisexuality, or from issues related to their or their partner's stage of sexual identity development. Common erroneous assumptions are that all bisexual people need both male and female partners to be satisfied or that, given the choice, they would prefer the privileged status of other-sex relationships. Lesbian or gay partners may worry, "Can I meet her/his needs?" or "Will she/he leave me for the other sex?" They might interpret bisexual identification as a threat to the relationship and wish for their partners to claim lesbian or gay identity to signify commitment.

The understandable importance of the solidarity of the subculture to the development and safety of many lesbian women and gay men can have the effect of reinforcing the dichotomous view of sexual orientation. Having suffered from oppression in a homophobic society, they may be suspicious of those who have access to the dominant culture. They may believe that bisexuality is only a transitional phase in the development of a gay or lesbian identity (perhaps based on their own experience). Or they may have difficulty believing in the reality of bisexuality and, thus, lack empathy for their partner's bisexuality.

Partner's Disclosure

Being in a relationship with someone who is in the early stages of bisexual identity development can be especially challenging. While a partner is grappling with the meaning and expression of her or his bisexuality, the lesbian woman or gay man must contend with insecurities about the future of the relationship, jealousy, condemnation from the community, and lack of access to helpful models and resources.

COUPLES' ISSUES

Some of the issues bisexual women and men and their lesbian or gay partners bring to therapy are relational issues, regardless of sexual orientation, such as communication; personality styles and interactions; physical, emotional, intellectual, spiritual, and sexual levels of connection. Some are issues that are not exclusive to these couples but take on a particular significance due to the difference in sexual orientation, such as safer sex, an affair, or monogamy versus polyamory. The issue of safer sex, for instance, can be especially charged between two women when one is bisexual and has a history of unprotected sex with men, or when they are exploring a sexually open relationship that may include men. The betrayal of a sexual affair can be aggravated by the discovery that it was with someone of the other sex, with whom a partner feels she or he cannot "compete." The subject of polyamory may arise as an attempt to accommodate a bisexual partner's needs rather than as a mutual lifestyle choice.

Issues Specific to Bisexuality

Those concerns that are directly related to one partner's bisexuality can stem from that person's newly discovered or newly acted upon other-sex attractions, or from a lack of clear understanding and communication between partners regarding the nature of the person's bisexuality. Couples often need education, resources, and help articulating their experiences and negotiating their way through decisions, once bisexuality becomes an issue in the relationship. When a bisexual partner is struggling with the meaning of her or his new awareness of dual attractions or is drawn to experiment with other-sex relationships, the couple is likely to be in distress and their attachment threatened. If a partner's bisexuality is not a new discovery but has never been fully discussed or accepted, there may be layers of misunderstandings, fears, or resentments that need exploration.

CASE EXAMPLES

Two examples of same-sex couples for whom bisexuality has been an issue in therapy will illustrate some of the problems brought to couple therapy and illuminate the discussion of therapeutic tasks to follow.

1. Sal had been out as lesbian since early adolescence, and Ronnie had been identified as a bisexual woman for several years before meeting her. Ronnie's continuing to identify as bisexual after entering into their relationship was taken by Sal as distancing, invalidating of the relationship, evidence of resistance to commitment, and generally threatening. Ronnie, who felt fully committed to the relationship, thought that calling herself lesbian would not be true to herself and would be inaccurate and invalidating. But she was conflicted over the pull from her partner and circle of friends to accept a lesbian identity, a pressure reinforced by her family, who found it easier to embrace a lesbian identity than a bisexual one. So she kept quiet.

When they had entered couple therapy at the beginning of their relationship to work on conflicts arising from their newly shared living situation, the therapist had referred to them as "lesbians," making an assumption based on appearances. This had the effect of silencing Ronnie, who knew her bisexual identity was problematic for Sal and did not want to increase the level of tension. They did receive help from this therapy in terms of communication, negotiation, and listening skills. But bisexuality was never discussed, and the issue continued unresolved, avoided by both in the interest of preserving the relationship. When they went to another therapist two years later because of increased arguments and dissatisfaction with their sex life, the therapist began by collecting history and identifying information, including sexual identity. Noting that this was a mixed-orientation relationship, the therapist asked how they experienced that, observed conflict and discomfort, and made room for them to express and examine their feelings about it. The issue could then become a focus of the work while they explored their concerns, assumptions, reactions, and needs together.

2. Rafael was a man who had had intimate relationships with women and men before meeting Sam, a gay man. They fell in love and chose each other as

life partners, agreeing to a relationship open to casual sexual encounters that did not include emotional closeness. Those encounters had been few for both and all with men. They sought couples therapy after Rafael expressed a strong attraction to a woman and began a relationship with her that included both sexual and emotional closeness. Sam was frightened that he would lose Rafael and angry at this change in their contract. He wondered whether Rafael was reacting to homophobia and unable to accept being gay. Rafael hoped there was a way he could ensure the security of his commitment to Sam, which was primary for him, while making room for a secondary relationship that fulfilled the different sexual and emotional needs he had for women. Couples therapy was an opportunity for them to reaffirm their bond, to examine the meaning of Rafael's bisexuality, to explore options for handling this crisis, to discuss their feelings about polyamory, and to renegotiate the structure of their relationship.

THERAPEUTIC TASKS

Acknowledging the Context of Oppression

The most important therapeutic task in working with these couples may be situating their problems in the appropriate context. Hardy (1997) has eloquently illustrated the necessity of addressing the psychological effects of oppression when working with marginalized clients. After years of adaptation to living with stigmatized identities in a homophobic, biphobic, and heterosexist culture, members of a lesbian-bi or gay-bi couple may no longer be fully aware of the impact of oppression on their lives and relationship. The couples therapist, in holding the assumption that homophobia and biphobia are underlying factors in their difficulties, can help the partners locate their problems in the cultural context and relieve some of the blame and pressure that falls on the individuals and the relationship. Throughout the therapy, it is important to attend to the issues of difference and oppression.

Because therapy may be the only or one of the few places a same-sex, mixed-orientation couple can experience acceptance and affirmation, the therapist's support for the relationship is vital. She or he can reflect the strengths each partner brings to the relationship and their commitment to working on a partnership despite the lack of familial, community, or societal support. Qualities they may have developed in forming their sexual and gender identities and in living in a nontraditional relationship (such as resilience, self-reliance, independence, respect for diversity, and empathy) can be highlighted to help them deal with the differences, stresses, social pressures, and conflicts that arise now.

Assessment

Therapy, of course, begins with assessment. As in all couple therapy, it is helpful to assess the partner's expectations, both positive and negative, their strengths, their coping ability, and their support system. However, these aspects of their personalities and lives take on a complexity for mixed-orientation couples. The therapist can help them gain perspective on their relationship while assessing their needs in therapy by asking specific questions, such as: What had they imagined being in a relationship with a bisexual/lesbian/gay partner might be like? What is positive about being with such a partner? What is difficult? What works well about their particular combination? How do they handle the problems with it? How many other couples like them do they know? How do their friends and families respond to their partnership?

A crucial consideration for bi-lesbian and bi-gay couples is developmental stage–that of their individual sexual identities, as well as that of their relationship. There have been several studies describing proposed stages in the development of lesbian and gay identity and long-term relationships that are helpful guides in this assessment (e.g., Cass, 1990; Chapman & Brannock, 1987; McWhirter & Mattison, 1985; Minton & McDonald, 1983/1984; Plummer, 1981; Troiden, 1988). It is important to determine, for instance, whether a lesbian or gay partner is struggling with her or his sexual identity, is exploring it for the first time, is in process of coming out, or has accepted or fully integrated it. Likewise, it is significant if the couple is in the intense first months of falling in love, is establishing a home together, or has spent years raising a family together.

Sexual identity development for bisexuals appears to be similar to, though more complex and less linear than lesbian/gay identity development. It is complicated by dualistic thinking and the lack of models or validation (Coleman, 1987; Shively & De Cecco, 1977; Rust, 1992). Bisexual women and men often begin by questioning the reality of their dual attractions and struggling with doubt about the meaning of their experience. Once having accepted the validity of their experience, they must create an identity for themselves that is not mirrored in the culture. Then having established it, they face the ongoing task of maintaining a bisexual identity despite constant encounters with isolation and invisibility (Bradford, 1997). Clearly, a bisexual partner's beginning to question her or his other-sex attractions will have a different impact on a relationship than one's needing support and validation for maintaining an ongoing identity.

Clarifying Meanings of Bisexuality

A task that the couples therapist can be especially helpful with is clarifying and articulating the bisexual partner's personal definition of bisexuality. There are many, varied individual definitions of bisexuality. For some, bisexuality means having a history of intimacy with both sexes, often with some prefer-ence, but with clear choice of exclusivity with the present partner. For others, it means feeling unfulfilled without relationships with both sexes. And some are in the process of discovering the meaning for themselves, but may wish to ask their partners to stand by them while they explore. One or both partners may need education regarding the myths and stereotypes and truths about bi-sexuality.

The therapist plays an important role in providing acceptance and affirma-tion for bisexuality, serving to counteract bisexual invisibility, while facilitat-ing an exploration of both partner's feelings and needs. Also valuable is a knowledge of resources, including books, journals, internet sites, local com-munity centers, and support groups.[1]

Facilitating Negotiations

Couple therapy may include consideration of issues of polyamory if perti-nent, with accompanying discussion of structure, limits, trust, jealousy, and safer sex. Negotiating consensual nonmonogamy requires clarifying each partner's motivations, needs, fears, expectations, and assumptions. A success-ful outcome demands of the partners a significant level of maturity, self-awareness, and well-developed communication skills. Of course, if this issue arises as a result of a breach, such as an affair, lying, and discovery, the work must begin with reconciliation and repairing of broken trust, and focus on de-termining the foundation and strengths of the relationship and redrawing the contract.

CONCLUSION

Bisexuality for one or both partners in a same-sex couple may not be an is-sue in the relationship. It may be only a fact to be recognized, acknowledged, and validated by the therapist. For those couples for whom it is problematic, clarification of meaning, exploration of assumptions and expectations, negoti-ation of differences, education, and referral to resources are all vital compo-nents of valuable therapy. Mixed-orientation couples often come into therapy so influenced by cultural stereotypes and prejudice as to assume their relation-ships are problematic. Therapy can provide them with safety and affirmation.

Lesbian women and gay men must form their sense of self and their rela-tionships in an atmosphere of homophobia, often without support of family, church, or government. Withstanding such pressure requires inner strength and self-confidence. Forming and maintaining a bisexual identity in a sexually dichotomous culture is a complex and difficult task that calls for resilience and self-reliance to counter the endemic isolation and invalidation. These qualities are positive strengths that enhance relationship. In reflecting this to the couple, the therapist assists them in drawing on their strengths to meet the challenges of their relationship.

NOTE

1. A good place to begin a search of bisexual resources is Ochs, R. (Ed.). (2001). *Bisexual resource guide* (4th ed.). Cambridge, MA: Bisexual Resource Center (www.bire source.org).

REFERENCES

Bradford, M. (1997). The bisexual experience: Living in a dichotomous culture (Doctoral dissertation, The Fielding Institute). *Dissertation Abstracts International, 58* (03B), 1520.

Cass, V. C. (1990). The implications of homosexual identity formation for the Kinsey model and scale of sexual preference. In D. P. McWhirter, S. A. Sanders, & J. M. Reinisch (Eds.), *Homosexuality/heterosexuality: Concepts of sexual orientation* (pp. 239-266). New York: Oxford University Press.

Chapman, B. E., & Brannock, J. C. (1987). Proposed model of lesbian identity development: An empirical examination. *Journal of Homosexuality, 14* (3/4), 69-80.

Coleman, E. (1987). Assessment of sexual orientation. *Journal of Homosexuality, 14* (1/2), 9-24.

Hardy, K. V. (1997, January). Not quite home: The psychological effects of oppression. *In the Family*, 7-8, 24.

Hutchins, L., & Kaahumanu, L. (Eds.). (1991). *Bi any other name: Bisexual people speak out*. Boston: Alyson Publications, Inc.

Kinsey, A. C., Pomeroy, W. B., & Martin, C. E. (1948). *Sexual behavior in the human male*. Philadelphia: W. B. Saunders Company.

Kinsey, A. C., Pomeroy, W. B., Martin, C. E., & Gebhard, P. H. (1953). *Sexual behavior in the human female*. Philadelphia: W. B. Saunders Company.

Klein, F., Sepekoff, B., & Wolf, T. J. (1985). Sexual orientation: A multi-variable dynamic process. *Journal of Homosexuality, 11* (1/2), 35-50.

Matteson, D. R. (1996). Counseling and psychotherapy with bisexual and exploring clients. In B. A. Firestein (Ed.), *Bisexuality: The psychology and politics of an invisible minority* (pp. 185-213). Thousand Oaks, CA: Sage Publications.

McWhirter, D. P., & Mattison, A. M. (1985). Psychotherapy for gay male couples. In J. C. Gonsiorek (Ed.), *A guide to psychotherapy with gay and lesbian clients* (pp. 79-91). New York: Harrington Park Press.

Minton, H. L., & McDonald, G. L. (1983/1984). Homosexual identity formation as a developmental process. *Journal of Homosexuality, 9* (2/3), 91-104.

Plummer, K. (1981). Going gay: Identities, life cycles and lifestyles in the male gay world. In J. Hart & D. Richardson (Eds.), *The theory and practice of homosexuality* (pp. 93-110). London: Routledge & Kegan Paul.

Rust, P. C. (1992). Who are we and where do we go from here: Conceptualizing bisexuality. In E. R. Weise (Ed.), *Closer to home: Bisexuality and feminism* (pp. 281-310). Seattle, WA: Seal Press.

Rust, P. C. (1995). *Bisexuality and the challenge to lesbian politics: Sex, loyalty, and revolution*. New York: New York University Press.

Rust, P. C. (1996). Managing multiple identities: Diversity among bisexual women and men. In B. A. Firestein (Ed.), *Bisexuality: The psychology and politics of an invisible minority* (pp. 53-83). Thousand Oaks, CA: Sage Publications.

Shively, M. & De Cecco, J. (1977). Components of sexual identity. *Journal of Homosexuality, 3* (1), 41-48.

Troiden, R. R. (1988). *Gay and lesbian identity: A sociological analysis.* Dix Hills, NY: General Hall, Inc.

Supporting Transgender
and Sex Reassignment Issues:
Couple and Family Dynamics

Gianna E. Israel

SUMMARY. For the care provider unfamiliar with supporting transsexual and transgender persons, as well as their partners, it becomes an imperative to be able to identify this population's unique needs, transition concerns and relationship dynamics. New challenges arise as transgender clients become more prevalent within the GLBT community and contact community clinical resources. These include distinguishing between sexual orientation and the complexities of gender identity; differentiating actual transgender issues and ordinary relationship concerns; and recognizing characteristics of strong relationships versus those doomed to fail when one or both partner's needs can no longer get met.

This article reviews an abundance of stereotypes adversely affecting transgender individuals, relationships and which can taint the treatment

Gianna E. Israel is a Gender-Specialized Community Counselor and author. Ms. Israel has provided nationwide telephone consultation, individual and relationship counseling, and gender specialized evaluations and recommendations since 1988. She is principal book author of *Transgender Care* with Donald Tarver, M.D. (Temple University Press/1997). She is a current HBIGDA member and former founding AEGIS board member.

Address correspondence to: Gianna E. Israel, P.O. Box 424447, San Francisco, CA 94142. (E-mail at Gianna@counselsuite.com). Contact by phone: (415) 558-8058. Her library is at (http://www.counselsuite.com).

[Haworth co-indexing entry note]: "Supporting Transgender and Sex Reassignment Issues: Couple and Family Dynamics." Israel, Gianna E. Co-published simultaneously in *Journal of Couple & Relationship Therapy* (The Haworth Press) Vol. 3, No. 2/3, 2004, pp. 53-63; and: *Relationship Therapy with Same-Sex Couples* (ed: Jerry J. Bigner, and Joseph L. Wetchler) The Haworth Press, Inc., 2004, pp. 53-63. Single or multiple copies of this article are available for a fee from The Haworth Document Delivery Service [1-800-HAWORTH, 9:00 a.m. - 5:00 p.m. (EST). E-mail address: docdelivery@haworthpress.com].

environment. At a core level, there exists the need for care providers to recognize when having a transgender identity stops being a disorder, such as when the client is no longer gender dysphoric, and where the care provider needs to advocate the individual's right of self-determination. This includes recognizing when situational depression or anxiety and social discrimination are the actual root of ongoing individual and relationship concerns. With basic transgender knowledge, effectively supporting transgender persons and their relationships is possible for cross-specialty providers, and is recommended. *[Article copies available for a fee from The Haworth Document Delivery Service: 1-800-HAWORTH. E-mail address: <docdelivery@haworthpress.com> Website: <http://www.Haworth Press.com> © 2004 by The Haworth Press, Inc. All rights reserved.]*

KEYWORDS. Transsexual, transgender, gender, couples, relationship, dysphoria

Imagine for a moment if you can, the profound confusion and distress an individual might experience looking into a mirror and seeing an opposite-gendered person staring back. Consider also not being able to determine whether one is a gay male or straight female, or perhaps, a lesbian woman or straight man! The preceding characterizes the discomfort which can arise for transsexual and other transgender persons dealing with gender dysphoria (Brown & Rounsley, 1996). It is one among many issues transgender people and their partners must contend with.

For counselors and therapists who provide services to same sex couples, transgender issues are becoming required knowledge as transfolk take on more pronounced visibility and interaction with the GLBT communities. With this development careproviders are asking questions. Possibly the most immediate concern clinicians have is differentiating between various transgender populations.

How is the professional supposed to define where a client is in transition, support that process, and still take into account a broadening array of transgender identities? Common sense would indicate that left unanswered such a clinical dilemma points to the reason that transgender men and women are so frequently turned away by providers. To determine what is going on with the client one simply needs ask. Spend time helping the client focus and share a personal and basic gender history. Then, look for patterns of consistency in the past and the present. It would also be helpful to ask what name and pronouns that person prefers. The longer an individual uses a "preferred" name, at least within discreet relationships, the more firmly grounded is the evolving gender identity.

Once it has been ruled out that the transgender client is not suffering from psychosis or another thought-impairing malady, it becomes possible to consider what issues the individual is presently experiencing and which are most affecting a couple's relationship (Israel & Tarver, 1997). If the person's main focus is to live "in role" at least part time and has chosen a preferred name, he or she may be either a *transsexual* or *transgenderist* (Israel, 1996). In other words, surgery is not an important issue at present, but developing a significant cross gender role and public presentation definitely is. If the transgender person expresses a consistent intention to undergo Genital Reassignment Surgery, and has a well-developed plan for it, that individual is likely a *transsexual*. It is these persons who fall under the larger transgender umbrella. Based on my clinical experience, it is these persons who are also most likely to make it into the office of a same sex counselor. These clients may emerge from either gay or straight communities.

A person's community of origin prior to coming to terms with gender issues can play an important role in how both the couple and transgender individual deal with relationship issues. For instance, *heterosexual crossdressers* are the least likely to seek individual or couple counseling. When they do, a strong emphasis on heterosexuality and short term work prevails with a focus on validation and cohesiveness (Miller, 1996). On the other hand, persons whose origin is the gay/lesbian community will be more cognizant of minority issues. They are generally more self-aware and more likely to address a broader spectrum of issues in counseling.

In review, we have covered those persons that definitely believe they want surgery, transsexuals; those individuals that definitely want to live in role part or full time, transsexuals and transgenderists; and crossdressers who dress for erotic satisfaction or social activities but don't care to live "in role" or alter their bodies. This essentially covers basic transgender populations. Other persons who self-identify as transgender will have similar needs. It also should be remembered that the label transgender is a sociopolitical construct–not a diagnosis. If the individual is gender dysphoric then Gender Identity Disorder is the correct diagnosis. However, when dysphoria is resolved and the person self identifies as transgender, it may be more appropriate to refer to whatever mental health symptoms linger as the diagnosis. Insurance billing should be discussed with the client, since not all individuals or couples are "out" to their employer, and may not want gender-related diagnoses appearing on statements (Israel & Tarver, 1997).

Before moving into a discussion of sexual orientation and how it may shift for transitioning persons, a definition for gender identity is required. *Gender identity* is not solely the masculinity or femininity a person feels on the inside, it is also how one portrays this to the world and how others mirror it back to the individual. This is critical knowledge for clinicians who come into contact with transgender persons. The heart of the gender conflict or dysphoria is that the person is often desperate for respect of his or her self-identification including the gender identity component. Until individuals are able to find support for their self-determined gender identity, there usually will be major social and interpersonal conflict.

During evaluation if it becomes apparent that the gender identity of pre-transition individuals is uncertain or immature, it often is and this is typically the case for sexual orientation as well. The stronger a cross-gender identification is, the more likely that individual will have to reassess and redefine his or her sexual orientation if a transition is to be made. In a survey of clients in my practice, approximately fifty-percent of persons who transition gender will reconsider who they prefer for a sex partner. It is also not uncommon for two transgender persons to be attracted, form a relationship, and benefit from each other's insights of a shared situation.

A RELATIONSHIP IN TURMOIL

Jan, a 43-year-old, male-to-female (MTF) pre-operative transsexual and Evelyn a 48-year-old, genetic woman have been married for eleven years. The couple sought couple counseling to help Evelyn better understand Jan's evolving gender identity.

Like many transsexuals, Jan had felt gender-conflicted since early childhood. Jan's first marriage was ended when her spouse found out about her transsexualism. Consequently Jan told Evelyn that she had these feelings at the onset of their relationship. For a number of years the couple had lived together as man and wife, and Evelyn secretly hoped the marriage would prevent Jan from transitioning. But, as is often the case, having a "normal" relationship was not sufficient to deter Jan from eventually coming to terms with her transsexualism.

Jan is now living full-time as a woman. Does that make her and Evelyn a lesbian couple? Jan also had uncertainties about undergoing genital reassignment because she feared major surgery. Conflicted, she also wasn't sure if she was attracted to men or women as a newly identified woman. Additionally, shortly after starting hormone therapy, she and Evelyn stopped having sexual intercourse. Though this couple is intimate, in the sense of heavy petting and kissing, both wondered if they would be able to sexually satisfy each other since hormones had diminished Jan's sex drive.

Several foundations exist which are critical to providing basic support to couples in which one partner has a transgender identity. These include encouraging clients to self-define their own gender identity and sexual orientation even if those definitions contradict social norms (Cromwell, 1999). It is also important to preserve the original caring which made their relationship develop. Finally, it behooves partners to learn as much as they can about transgender issues before making any significant plans or changes.

Before we can consider relationships which endure, an overview of reasons why such relationships fail is required knowledge. The actions that most radically destabilize relationships are the transgender partner's coming-out privately and publicly; starting hormones; and preparing for and undergoing various expensive cosmetic and genital reassignment surgical procedures. This is true whether a partner decides to live part-time in role, or permanently. Because pursuing a well-planned transition takes months, this actually gives the couple considerable opportunity to develop plans for safeguarding each other's welfare. If both parties are wise enough to fully exploit this window of opportunity both can benefit.

The most destructive blow occurs when a spouse, stereotypically a heterosexual woman, reactively abandons the relationship or evicts the transgender-identified partner from the family home. This overreaction is traumatizing for all parties involved, spouses and children (Brown & Rounsley, 1996). Dramatic endings are less common for heterosexual males. Those men with a newly identified female-to-male (FTM) partner tend to move more slowly in the task of termination and rebuilding their lives. In situations where a couple is originally gay or lesbian identified, both tend to move in a more circumspect fashion and often remain close friends and allies. The commonest dynamics which characterize the non-transgender partner's response follow.

"Denial" is a word that speaks volumes. Unlike those who terminate a relationship immediately, there are also spouses who don't even want to deal with the gender issue.

Some are likely to pretend nothing will change for as long as possible. Initially this works well, allowing a transitioning person to complete electrolysis and build skills in his or her new role. But, long-term denial doesn't allow the non-transgender partner to prepare for his or her future. Often the non-transgender partner will engage in passive-aggressive behavior and manipulation.

Up until the present, this article has dealt with examples in which most relationships will end or develop termination plans. Generally this occurs soon after discovery that a partner is transgender or discloses an intention to transition. But, termination does not always have to be the end result. In some instances couples stay together for years and exemplify great relationship skills, cohesiveness and deep caring. There are also persons emerging from gay or lesbian relationships, who are not interested in transition or surgeries, but instead expect to be accepted as a "new man" or "new woman." This trend demands further inquiry as such couples become increasingly evident. Whatever a person's gender identification and sexual orientation, however, the best that care providers can do is facilitate the individuals' meeting each other's needs or explore moving on in a measured fashion.

While coming to terms with the gender issue, many partners will feel deeply betrayed. This most often occurs when the transgender person did not have the communication skills to disclose earlier in the relationship. Sometimes it takes years for the transgender person to learn how to tell another person about his or her gender dysphoria (Cromwell, 1999). Whereas the issue of loss may take months, even years, to process, a failure to disclose early exacerbates issues of trust and guilt. This is true whether or not the relationship remains intact.

What may come as a surprise to some careproviders, but not to most separating couples, gender issues are often not the only problem though it may be the catalyst for termination (Brown & Rounsley, 1996). In a general sense within relationships partners see what they want in each other. However, if the relationship does not evolve and mature at some juncture the illusions shatter, leaving behind communication impasses, domestic conflicts and intimacy difficulties.

During counseling it is not uncommon for individuals or couples to demand a care provider's projection about whether a relationship is doomed to fail. Has intimacy died? Does more fighting occur? Or, is it possible to overcome core problems and reestablish a fulfilling companionship? Much will depend on whether the ability to fulfill each other's needs and a strong investment in the relationship exists. Care providers need to be mindful of these dynamics and not yield to the temptation of predicting a relationship's outcome. Instead, they should teach clients to draw their own conclusions and make informed decisions.

Nothing exemplifies a relationship's character better than how a couple handles issues involving children. Like gay and lesbian parents, transgender mothers and fathers face enormous social hostilities based on stereotypes (Cromwell, 1999). Often these can be introduced into the situation by the non-transgender spouse. I have observed within my clinical practice that GLBT persons are capable of being good parents. Many are great, actually. Regrettably, this rarely is publicized with society at large, and for many non-transgender parents, a partner's transitioning will inspire an abundance of fear. For instance, many of these fears are a result of never actually having met transgender persons who are parents. Referring such couples to groups which include transgender parents can be a helpful intervention (Israel & Tarver, 1997).

Sometimes, parents will have very basic questions. Does exposure to a transgender parent or person mean that a child will become transgendered? No. Do young children adjust to a parent changing gender? The majority can, particularly in families where respecting differences in other people is a value. Should a child call his or her parent by a certain name, title or pronoun? No. Children will always see the father as their father, or the mother as their mother. Only with maturity and social sophistication will they learn to use vocabulary appropriate to the transgender parent's presentation.

The vast majority of children adjust very well to having a transgender parent. As long as children are reassured that the gender conflict is the parent's issue, and are taught how to deal with peer harassment, most children will be satisfied with basic, honest answers to their gender related questions. Otherwise, as with most young persons, they will mature and develop interests or agendas of their own. Many of the parent's issues are destined to become non-issues to children.

In working with both individuals and couples, I strongly encourage the transgender parent not to look to their children as a primary source of gender validation. The transitioning person is responsible for gaining his or her validation from adult sources, such as adult friends, family and a support network (Israel & Tarver, 1997). Children always should be allowed to develop acceptance on their own terms. In other words, simply because a young daughter enjoys shopping for women's clothes with an male-to-female (MTF) parent, that young child still sees the individual as her father. It may be some years before that changes, even though outwardly she may say otherwise to please the parent.

In counseling, couples should also be reminded that children generally come from the parents caring for each other. Again, we return to the concept that both parents need to respect the caring which served as an original foundation for their relationship. Children need to see how loving, mature people act toward each other. When this doesn't occur the likelihood significantly increases that the child will reject one or both parents. It is common for children of all ages to deal with issues of denial, fear and loss when a parent discloses his or her gender issues. When healthy coping mechanisms are not promoted, however, children are all the more likely to adopt the credo of their peers, which is generally to reject anything that is different or frightening.

Moving ahead to a new focus, genital reassignment surgery is usually seen as the end-stage of a person dealing with his or her transsexualism (Miller, 1996). Be forewarned, that it is not. Surgical candidates are expected to have lived legally in-role full time for at least one year, as well as having undergone hormone administration, cosmetic procedures and been occupied with employment, volunteer activities or school as a new man or woman. Transsexual clients are often unaware of how critical socialization is in all stages of transition in order to be well-adjusted post-operatively. Persons interested in pertinent clinical reading on male-to-female (MTF) and female-to-male (FTM) surgical procedures, experiences and protocols may do so in the *Transgender Care* book (Israel/Tarver, MD–Temple University Press, 1997).

The impact of genital reassignment affects a couple's relationship in many ways. Beyond the financial expense which is sometimes born by both partners, there is also a high emotional toll. When a couple remains together, or at least maintains a friendship, the non-transgender partner often will be asked to lend comfort during the surgical partner's post-operative recovery. Many do so willingly, bringing each closer together and giving additional meaning to the transition experience (Brown & Rounsley, 1996). Nevertheless, dealing with major surgery and recovery creates a great deal of anticipatory anxiety for both.

Post-operatively, if the couple is to be sexually intimate, it is necessary that they redefine what is sexually satisfying for each of them. In many cases, referring back to the evolving sexual orientation issue, the post-operative transsexual will have a healthy desire to explore his or her new genitalia and sex roles (Israel & Tarver, 1997). This may present conflicts in a monogamous relationship or at a minimum introduce unfulfilled desires which can prove challenging.

REFUND REQUESTED!

Ivy, a 43-year-old, genetic woman, has had a continuous relationship for 17 years with Heather, a 39 year old, post-operative transsexual woman. Ivy coaxed her partner into couple counseling, even though she suspected Heather needed individual therapy. In session, both of the women agreed they had been through a lot together and had much invested in their relationship. For instance, Ivy had held Heather's hand after her partner underwent genital reassignment fifteen years ago. Since then the couple had purchased a house and were established participants in the local women's community.

At issue for Ivy was Heather's behavior during the past 18 months. As a couple both were secure financially. However, Heather had lost her job and refused to look for work. Additionally, she had completely let her appearance deteriorate. In street terms she looked "tore up" in fact, more and more like a man. This was so even though Heather claimed to have no intention to reverting to a masculine role. Ivy felt frustrated because she invested herself into a lesbian relationship only to find herself with a woman that looked more male than female.

To add to the couple's difficulties Heather was staying up all night, which conflicted with Ivy's schedule. Heather also frequently refused to eat and was so moody it became nearly impossible for Ivy to talk to her without an argument occurring.

The couple's counselor in this scenario had never worked with a lesbian couple in which one partner was a post-operative or "post-op" transsexual. Was the surgery a mistake? Probably not. Did Heather need to have her hormone levels checked through blood laboratory testing to insure she was receiving the right medication? Yes. Of more concern, was Heather afflicted with depression? Perhaps so.

Abandoning a transition or "reverting role" is a fairly common phenomena among pre- and post-operative transsexuals and other transgender persons when mental illness strikes. It can undermine a person's efforts to build self confidence and establish a stable gender identity. Reverting is also very confusing to the loved ones, friends and careproviders who supported the person's transition.

As the preceding case scenario *"Refund Requested"* portrays, a close examination of actual symptoms will reveal underlying mental disorders. Is it possible to address mental illness early enough to prevent reversion and other types of deterioration? Generally, yes. The wisest course in the preceding scenario is to direct the transgender partner into individual therapy and schedule a blood laboratory/medication check-up, so that his or her comfort levels can be increased regardless of whether lingering gender issues remain (Israel & Tarver, 1997). The reality is the longer a person lives in role, and we refer to "years" in most cases, the less likely a permanent reversion will occur. After all, transgender persons aren't the only ones who allow their circumstances and appearances to deteriorate when suffering mental illness.

The preceding scenario also introduces an ethical issue relevant to providing transgender care. Should the counselor who sees the couple also see the transgender person individually? In the best of circumstances, the answer is no. Doing so may give a misleading impression that the therapist is an ally of one of the clients. Therefore, it would be more effective to have one therapist for the couple and an individual care provider to help the transgender client deal with gender and mental health issues.

Unfortunately, many communities may have a paucity of gender specialists. Less cosmopolitan areas may have few if any clinicians willing to see transgender clients. Also, the cost of having a counselor for each family member may be prohibitive. What should be done in a situation where the specialist or gender-supportive counselor is faced with multiple demands? Where there is a dearth of local resources it is reasonable to determine where the providers skills would meet the most critical needs. This could be either the individual and/or couple, whichever is determined to be most at risk.

While no transgender person should ever do without mental health care, many individuals are capable of managing large aspects of transition using nationwide resources, support groups and friends. In a similar vein, it is also possible for a couple to reach mutually healthy decisions and grow while dealing with gender issues. This is particularly so if the transgender person is adequately educated and able to inform his or her partner of what lays ahead (Brown & Rounsley, 1996).

Staying together can have a positive impact on a couple's relationship. During transition and afterward growth is possible. A couple's ability to communicate can improve as a result of dealing with complex gender issues. Many partners will report that much self blame was experienced in their relationship prior to transition, but that this eventually resolved as each confronted the other's vulnerability. It is also possible that one or both partners will become more socially outgoing. Dealing with gender issues requires enormous creativity; consequently, partners find themselves relaxing overly rigid boundaries, expectations and stereotypes (Cromwell, 1999).

Dealing with gender identity issues through and after transition requires a massive psychological effort for the transgender person to attain a semblance of normalcy. This can also be true for the long-term partner of such a person. This is a dynamic which should not be ignored. Instead the couple's counselor should highlight it as one of the relationship's strengths. There certainly are no right or wrong answers for approaching transgender issues when a couple strives to make a relationship work. What hopefully becomes evident with their efforts is a continuous, healthy relationship.

COMMON TRANSGENDER STEREOTYPES

Popular fallacies can create treatment impediments for any population, and this includes transgender persons and their partners. Even the most seasoned gender specialist must strive against falling prey to assumptions about a client's experiences or imposing judgments on what should be a self-determination process (Israel & Tarver, 1997). Each of the following stereotypes are false and demystified below:

- *Transgender (TG) people are commonly viewed as mentally ill.* Once gender dysphoria resolves, however, having a TG identity becomes a matter of self-determination of gender identity, not an illness. There must be a consistent effort on the part of care providers to depathologize the transgender identity to clients, their partners and others.
- *TG people are believed to know of their gender identity early in life, such as in childhood.* In actuality some individuals may not become aware of it until mid- or late-life. There are also individuals who may spend large portions of their lives unaware that information about transgender persons or gender issues actually exist.
- *It is assumed that TG people typically want to end their current relationship once coming to terms with their identity has occurred.* Many, however, would remain in their current pre-transition relationship if the choice was up to them. Unfortunately, often this cannot occur because it is not always possible for every couple to meet each others needs.
- *TG people are permanently disowned by their entire family after coming out.* Actually, although some are disowned, the vast majority of TG persons are capable of maintaining or rekindling relationships as well as forming new ones. Exploring and understanding this process is critical to the success of the transitioning person, including those individuals who may temporarily lose family members. It may take some time, months or even years, for others to adjust to the transgender person's evolving identity and needs.
- *It is easy to predict how a TG person will dress and what type of occupation he or she will engage in.* This is incorrect. Many varieties of self expression exist for TG people, as with members of any community. TG persons are skilled and employed in all fields.
- *TG persons are perceived to live unhappy, unfulfilled or amoral lives.* This is a mischaracterization that is extended to many marginalized and subjugated populations. Even in the throes of gender dysphoria, it is pos-

sible for TG persons to experience joy, maintain positive goals and pursue a meaningful spiritual existence.

• *TG persons are believed to always be at risk of losing child custody and visitation rights.* In reality, by carefully presenting educational materials in family court, many TG persons have been able to secure their parental rights. Such an effort should be case managed by a gender specialist familiar with custody issues.

REFERENCES

Brown, M. & Rounsley, C. (1996). *True selves: Understanding transsexualism.* San Francisco: Jossey-Bass.

Cromwell, J. (1999), *Transmen and FTM's: Identities, bodies, genders and sexualities.* Urbana and Chicago: University of Illinois Press.

Israel, G. (1996), De Transgenderist: Als zelfidentificatie het opneemt tegen T & T–stereotypen. *Transformatie Journal.* (3-6) Amsterdam.(Transgenderists: When Self Identification Challenges Transgender Stereotypes) English version at http://www.firelily.com/gender/gianna/transgenderists.html

Israel, G. & Tarver, D. (1997), *Transgender care: Recommended guidelines, practical information, and personal accounts.* Philadelphia: Temple University Press.

Miller, N. (1996), *Counseling in genderland: A guide for you and your transgendered client.* Boston: A Different Path Press.

A Systems Approach
to Sex Therapy with Gay Male Couples

Michael Bettinger

SUMMARY. Sex therapy with gay male couples is difficult for many family and relationship therapists. Family therapists lack knowledge of the nature of sex therapy, gay male culture and sexuality, the dynamics of gay male couples, and the sexual issues gay male couples are likely to bring to sex therapy. Countertransference also makes sex therapy with gay male couples difficult for some family and relationship therapists. This paper addresses those issues and then explains a systems approach to sex therapy with gay male couples. *[Article copies available for a fee from The Haworth Document Delivery Service: 1-800-HAWORTH. E-mail address: <docdelivery@haworthpress.com> Website: <http://www.HaworthPress.com> © 2004 by The Haworth Press, Inc. All rights reserved.]*

Michael Bettinger, PhD, MFT, is a psychotherapist, author and educator in private practice in San Francisco. He is the author of *It's Your Hour: A Guide to Queer-Affirmative Psychotherapy*, published by Alyson Books of Los Angeles (E-mail: mcpsycle@well.com).

[Haworth co-indexing entry note]: "A Systems Approach to Sex Therapy with Gay Male Couples." Bettinger, Michael. Co-published simultaneously in *Journal of Couple & Relationship Therapy* (The Haworth Press) Vol. 3, No. 2/3, 2004, pp. 65-74; and: *Relationship Therapy with Same-Sex Couples* (ed: Jerry J. Bigner, and Joseph L. Wetchler) The Haworth Press, Inc., 2004, pp. 65-74. Single or multiple copies of this article are available for a fee from The Haworth Document Delivery Service [1-800-HAWORTH, 9:00 a.m. - 5:00 p.m. (EST). E-mail address: docdelivery@haworthpress.com].

65

KEYWORDS. Sex therapy, family therapy, gay male couples, gay men, homosexuality, sexuality, monogamy, countertransference, systems, growth model

Sex therapy with a gay male couple is a subset of family therapy and is different from sex therapy with an individual gay man. When working with an individual, the focus is often on symptoms that respond to a behaviorally oriented approach. When working with gay male couples, the focus is expanded to include the interpersonal aspects. This is best handled by a systems-oriented family therapist.

Sex therapy is a modality that is challenging for many family therapists (Mason, 1991). This is unfortunate because I believe many gay (and non-gay) couples would agree with the sentiment; "Sex may be only 10% of our relationship, but it is the first 10%." My experience is that family therapists do not pay sufficient attention to the sexual relationship of the couples with whom they are working. When listening to other family therapists present cases, I rarely hear them addressing how the interpersonal dynamics are affecting the couple's sex life. I believe this is even more likely to occur when working with gay male couples for the following reasons: therapists lack knowledge of gay male culture, the biases of the marriage and family profession concerning homosexuality and monogamy, countertransference issues and a general lack of understanding of the role of the family therapist in sex therapy.

All family therapists, gay and non-gay, need to be minimally competent to provide sex therapy services to gay male couples if they wish to work with gay male couples at all. This may seem debatable, but it shouldn't be. Sexual relations, or the lack thereof, is a major focus of all committed adult relationships. It is not good to think one can do couples counseling without thinking of oneself as capable of doing sex therapy with couples. They are closely tied.

While it might be appropriate for a family therapist to refer a gay man to a behaviorally oriented sex therapist to alleviate particular symptomology, the systemic issues, including the causes, the impact, and the resistance to change are best handled in couple counseling. The sexual issues may not always be the presenting problem. Often a gay male couple will start by talking about a communication problem, or a specific disagreement. Only after trust has been established will the couple begin to talk about the sexual problems. This necessitates that the family therapist be competent to handle this part of the work.

I do not classify myself as a sex therapist. I think of myself as a family therapist who happens to be a gay man, and one who deals with the sexual issues in couples and families. A family therapist does not have to become a specialist in sex therapy to work with many of the sexual issues gay male (or other) couples bring to the therapy room. This article is based on my 30 years of clinical experience as a family therapist working with gay men and gay male couples.

GAY MALE CULTURE, SEXUALITY AND RELATIONSHIPS

The Uniqueness of Gay Male Couple Culture

In order to work with gay male couples, a family therapist needs to be knowledgeable about gay male culture, particularly in the areas where the cultural values of gay men and family therapists conflict. Gay male culture is not monolithic. All gay men have strong identifications as members of other ethnic, religious, racial and economic groups. The knowledgeable family therapist uses his or her judgment to understand which of the sometime conflicting cultural values are affecting the couple. The following section explains some areas of gay male culture, sexuality and relationships which will help a family therapist who is interested doing sex therapy with gay male couples.

Gay Male Couple Sexuality

Gay male couples are composed only of men. While this may seem like a tautology, it contains an immense truth. From the time they are born, men are exposed to a multitude of messages encouraging them to be sexual. Gay men are firstly and primarily men. Gay male couples have a strong focus on sexuality because they are men.

Our society further emphasizes to gay men the sexual aspect of their nature and their committed adult relationships. Even this author finds it linguistically necessary to refer to these pairings as "gay" male couples, rather than simply as male couples. The repeated reference to the sexual nature of male/male relationships, absent in most references to male/female relationships focuses attention on the sexual part of the relationship.

Gay male couples, because they do not include a female perspective on sexuality, create relationships with typically male values toward sexuality. While there is a wide variation of values among gay men and couples, the resulting norms should be predictable to those familiar with typical male values toward sexuality.

For instance, the majority of all the stable, committed, long term gay male couples I have ever known began their relationship with a "one night stand." Gay men usually check out sexual compatibility early in their relationship. If there isn't sexual compatibility that first time, the relationship is unlikely to progress from there.

The cultural difference that is likely to be most difficult for family therapists concerns sexual monogamy. Coleman and Rosser (1996) indicate that gay male couples tend to be emotionally monogamous but not sexually monogamous. Blumstein and Schwartz (1983) found the longer a gay male couple is together, the less likely it is to be sexually monogamous. Within family therapy, the default is a bias toward monogamous relationships. Open relationships are looked upon as problematic, and the lack of a desire for monogamy is often interpreted as a sign of problems with intimacy.

For gay male couples, the default is a bias toward non-monogamy. While some gay male couples are monogamous, the majority are not (Blumstein & Schwartz, 1983). Gay couples handle the monogamy issue in different ways than do non-gay couples.

Many gay couples discuss the subject openly, agreeing to monogamy or non-monogamy. For others, these desires are communicated subtly. Discussing or renegotiating these agreements may be part of the work that a gay couple does in sex therapy.

Open relationships do not necessarily mean anything goes for gay male couples. Couples negotiate limits. One couple I know decided on an open relationship but each agreed to exclude anal sex with anyone else. For another couple the rule is "do not bring anyone home, and do not stay out all night." For still others, the rules involve limiting intimacy in those sex contacts, such as only outside sex in bathhouses or sex clubs, or no sex with anyone more than one time. For still others, it is situational. One can have sex with someone when one is out of town, or while on vacation. And for some couples it is OK to have a menage a trois, but not for either to have sex with someone else alone.

Gay Male Couple Dynamics

The non-monogamous nature of gay male relationships may lead a family therapist who is use to working with heterosexual couples to conclude that gay male relationships are not emotionally close or cohesive. But such an assumption would be badly mistaken, and interventions based on such an assumption would hinder the work with gay male couples.

While gay men fit the masculine stereotype regarding their pursuit of sexuality, gay men are quite different from heterosexual men in committed relationships. Gay men form emotionally close, cohesive relationships (Green, Bettinger, & Zacks, 1996). While lesbians form the closest relationships, gay men follow them in closeness. The most disengaged relationships are those formed by heterosexuals. The structural problems gay men have in relationship are more likely to come from too much enmeshment rather than from too much disengagement with each other.

Gay male couples also tend to form relationships that are more flexible and less rigid than are heterosexual relationships (Green et al., 1996). Roles and responsibilities are more likely to change. While there is the danger of chaos, the inherent flexibility in gay male relationships opens the couple to the possibility of changing those patterns that have become dysfunctionally rigid. And breaking rigid patterns is an important part of the work with gay male couples (Greenan & Tunnell, 2002).

In addition to monogamy, there are other common issues gay male couples may want to discuss in couples sex therapy. One is a decline in frequency or the disappearance of sex between the two, often for reasons not obvious to the couple. Sexual activity declines or disappears more rapidly in gay male couples than it does in heterosexual couples (Blumstein & Schwartz, 1983). Most of those men continue to have sexual relations with others. Often, the couple remains emotionally close and will want to discuss the lack of sexuality between them in couples sex therapy.

Another sexual issue gay male couples may want to discuss is the role each will take in sexual activity. Terms like "top" and "bottom," or "active" and "passive" are used to describe these roles. (These terms are misnomers since the one in the "top" role may not physically be on top, and the one in the "passive" role is rarely passive.) In oral or anal sex, for instance, the one doing the inserting is called the top or the active partner, and the one into whom the penis is being inserted is called the bottom or the passive partner.

In my personal experience, about one third of gay men prefer the top role, one third prefer the bottom role, and one third are versatile, meaning they enjoy being in both roles. (Both mainstream culture, and gay male culture to some extent devalues, stigmatizes and shames men who are in the bottom/passive role). Some gay male couples find themselves in a position where both men strongly prefer the same role, either top or bottom. And while these roles tend to be somewhat enduring, for some men they change, possibly destabilizing the sexual relationship.

Differences in HIV status can have a big impact on sexual functioning that could lead to problems. Some couples begin their relationship with this difference; for others one converts to being HIV positive during the relationship. While the primary mode of HIV transmission among gay men is unprotected receptive anal intercourse, most other forms of sexual contact contain some risk, though often low, of HIV transmission. The "safer" sex concept recognizes this risk may be managed but not eliminated. That risk potentially causes many sexual problems as it restricts or modifies various sexual practices, and working on this is a part of what may constitute sex therapy.

Medications can have an impact on gay male couple's sexual functioning. Depression is common among gay men (Ritter & Terndrup, 2002) and many have been prescribed antidepressant medication, causing a loss of libido, difficulty getting or maintaining erections or having orgasms. HIV antiviral medication often causes gastrointestinal upset, impacting desire as well as the mechanics of oral and anal sex. Recreational drugs, including methamphetamine often increase sexual desire but also cause performance problems. Couples may want to discuss these issues as part of sex therapy.

These are only some of the issues couples may want to discuss. Family therapists can further increase their knowledge of gay male culture in a number of ways. There is now a body of relevant professional literature on gay male relationships (the books and articles cited in the reference section of this article are a good beginning). One can also learn by reading gay male fiction and non-fiction, going to movies with themes related to gay male sexuality, reading home pages on the Internet, and by asking gay men to help educate you.

COUNTERTRANSFERENCE

Countertransference is a conscious and unconscious process resulting in the therapist experiencing positive, negative and/or neutral feelings in response to clients (Slakter, 1987). These feelings are based in the therapist's personal or familial experiences. Green and Mitchell (2002, p. 563) succinctly frame the countertransference issue by saying "The single, most important prerequisite for helping same-sex couples is the therapist's personal comfort with love and sexuality between two women or two men." Countertransference is an immense source of information for the therapist. A clinician therefore needs to be aware of his or her countertransference.

Many psychotherapists will experience discomfort when gay male couples discuss sexual practices and gay male clients recognize this. Gay men often have a finely tuned intuitive ability to sense a professional's discomfort or disapproval of their sexual choices. This is a healthy adaptive mechanism for gay men. Often psychotherapists are unaware that they are having a negative countertransference resulting in their being judgmental and unempathetic (Bettinger, 2002).

Several areas of discussion are more likely than others to bring out a negative countertransference on the part of the therapist. While it may not be possible for the therapist to avoid having a negative reaction, it is likely that the countertransference can be recognized, contained, and commented upon if necessary by the therapist. Areas with great potential for a negative countertransference are anal and oral sex, non-monogamous relationships, group sex, "kinky" sexual practices, "safer sex" issues and drug use during sex.

Working on Countertransference

A primer on gay male sexuality will enable a family therapist to become aware of his or her countertransference while reading this article. Gay male sexuality often involves direct contact between the penis, mouth or anus of one man, with the penis, mouth or anus of the other man. Add that the men also have hands, torsos and all other body parts, and the permutations of what is sexually possible begin to emerge in the readers mind. Stop, reread the preceding paragraph and contemplate what you have read.

As the reader contemplates the above paragraph, feelings are likely to have occurred. Were they positive or negative? How strong were they? Were any of the sexual acts difficult to contemplate? Was the thought of two men kissing difficult or appealing, comforting or appalling? What about oral sex? Anal sex? Oral/anal contact?

The reader should now have some idea as to his or her countertransference in relation to common gay male sexual acts, the discussion of which may be necessary during sex therapy. To continue the work, particularly when the countertransference was negative, I suggest the following exercise.

The following is a series of questions to help you to deal with your counter-transference. I ask you to read and think about your answers to these questions. If you are willing to do more work, I ask you to write your answers out. And, if it is possible to do so, I would encourage you to discuss these answers with your personal therapist or possibly your clinical consultant depending on the relationship you have with that individual. The goal will be to reach a point where you can think, write or talk about your thoughts, feelings, experiences, desires and fantasies regarding the following issues in a matter of fact way.

Regarding oral and anal sex: What are your personal experiences? Do you have any moral or religious feelings about either? Do you have any health concerns regarding those practices? Do you or have you fantasized about either? Does either cause you to feel uncomfortable?

Regarding non-monogamous relationships, I ask you to consider the following: Have you ever been in a non-monogamous relationship? Would you consider that under any circumstances? Have you, or a partner, ever "cheated" in a monogamous relationship? Who in your extended family of origin had sexual relations outside his or her committed relationship? How were those liaisons treated? Do you have any moral or religious feelings about non-monogamous relationships? Have you had any experiences, feelings or fantasies about having sex with more than one person at a time?

Discussion of "kinky" sexual practices is likely to bring up strong counter-transference feelings. While for some, kinky sex may bring up sadomasochistic images of whips and ropes, it actually exists along a continuum from mild to wild. Sexual variations may include role plays (cop/criminal, teacher/student, etc.), spankings, fetishes, paraphilias, cross dressing, involvement with bodily fluids, exhibitionism, voyeurism plus too many other variations to list here. After further educating yourself to understand what constitutes kinky sex, you should be able to think about, write or talk about your feelings, experiences, fantasies and fears regarding those practices.

With the advent of AIDS in the early 1980s, "safer sex" practices have been touted as one way of helping gay men and others to prevent the transmission of the disease. The most important of those practices is the use of condoms during anal or vaginal sex, primarily intended to prevent the transmission of HIV to the receptive one in that relationship. Think about the following: Do you or have you used condoms during sex? How was that experience for you? Did it change the nature or quality of the sexual relations for you, physically, mentally, romantically, or emotionally? How so? Would you encourage gay male couples to use condoms? Would you equally encourage heterosexual couples to use condoms?

Many gay male couples may want to include in the discussions of their sexuality the use of recreational drugs during sex. To what extent have you used drugs during sexual relations, including alcohol and caffeine? How did those substances change the experience for you? Have you, or any member of your family had any difficulty with the use of alcohol or drugs?

A positive countertransference can also be problematic. While the couple needs to feel that the therapist is in their corner, a positive countertransference might indicate an over identification with the couple or an erotic countertransference. Gay male couples are not monolithic. The therapist needs to be careful that he or she does not personally identify with the choices the couple is making. An erotic countertransference will impede the clinical judgment of the therapist.

One final note: a therapist is not expected to not have countertransference. He or she is only expected to recognize his or her countertransference, and to contain the countertransference as needed to minimize its impact on the work.

A SYSTEMS APPROACH TO SEX THERAPY WITH GAY MALE COUPLES

In providing sex therapy services to gay male couples, I use a systems approach based on the growth model (Bettinger, 2001). My experience has shown me that this is more effective than the more commonly used symptom approach based on a medical model.

The Growth Model

The systems approach of family therapy is based on the growth model. The growth model stipulates that we all function somewhere along a continuum from low to high functioning, and that we want to grow and increase our level of functioning. Often we develop rigid behavioral patterns, making change/ growth difficult. Many of these patterns (symptoms) have secondary gains, making them difficult to give up. The work in sex therapy is to help the couple (the system) break those patterns in order to establish a new homeostasis. Changes anywhere in the system will have repercussions in other parts of the system, giving the therapist many options for interventions. This is a holistic approach that takes into account the sexual symptoms presented by the couple, along side the entire picture of the couple's sexuality, within a frame of reference of the family system created by the couple.

It is helpful when conceptualizing the couple's issues to see the problematic symptom(s) presented by the couple as the "identified symptom(s)," much in the same way family therapists see the one experiencing it as the "identified patient."

Getting the Story

The family therapist should begin with an assessment, getting the personal and family history, as well as the individual sex history of both men. This should include family of origin attitudes toward sex, their coming out process, and the history of sexual relations between them.

That information should enable the therapist to arrive at an understanding of the big picture, including the presenting problems, sexual and non-sexual, and the general level of functioning of the couple, sexual and non-sexual. The overall objective is to raise both the general and sexual levels of functioning. This may, or may not include the elimination of a particular symptom. Sometimes symptoms can only be managed rather than be eliminated. The family therapist needs to understand where the symptoms fit into the big picture, and how well the couple is doing both on a sexual and non-sexual level. It is possible to increase the level of sexual and general functioning to a more satisfying level without changing the presenting symptom by changing other aspects of the system. And ultimately, all couples want to be higher functioning.

One technique I use is to get the "sex story" of the relationship. I ask each to tell me the sex story of the relationship, starting at the beginning. How did it begin (a one night stand, a dinner date)? What were/are the important elements (monogamy, oral sex, frequent sex, kinky sex, etc.)? What did it evolve to? To get the story and an understanding of the sexual level of functioning of the couple, a therapist needs to talk with them about sexual matters, at times explicitly. Here is where the work on countertransference will pay off.

This beginning phase is perhaps the most important part of the couple sex therapy work. It establishes a rapport and begins building trust between the couple and the family therapist. Sex and shame are closely linked in our culture, and gay men were and are constantly exposed to messages that say their sexual feelings and behaviors are shameful. By getting the sex story, discussions of sex is normalized and destigmatized.

From there the work is quite similar to generic couples work, only the content is the sexual relationship of the couple. The family therapist balances supporting and validating the couple and their sexual relationship while at the same time doing interventions designed to unbalance the dysfunctionally rigid parts of the system. Knowledge of gay male culture and personal comfort with sexuality make this easier.

ENDNOTE

While sex therapy with gay male couples may seem intimidating to the non-gay or inexperienced family therapist, it is something that can be learned. The key is in understanding gay male culture, one's own countertransference regarding gay male sexual issues and a systems approach to sex therapy. The family therapist will then be able to provide a needed service to a misunderstood minority.

REFERENCES

Bettinger, M. (2001). *It's your hour: A guide to queer affirmative psychotherapy.* Los Angeles: Alyson.

Bettinger, M. (2002). Sexuality, boundaries, professional ethics, and clinical practice: The kink community. *Journal of Gay & Lesbian Social Services 14* (4), 93-104.

Blumstein, P., & Schwartz, P. (1983). *American couples: Money, work and sex.* New York: William Morrow & Company.

Coleman, E. & Rosser, B. (1996). Gay and bisexual male sexuality. In R. Cabaj & T. Stein (Eds.) *Textbook of homosexuality and mental health* (pp. 707-721). Washington, D.C.: American Psychiatric Press, Inc.

Green, R-J., Bettinger, M., & Zacks, E. (1996). Are lesbian couples fused and gay male couples disengaged?: Questioning gender straightjackets. In J. Laird & R-J. Green (Eds.), *Lesbians and gays in couples and families: A handbook for therapists* (pp. 185-230). San Francisco: Jossey-Bass.

Green, R-J., & Mitchell, V. (2002). Gay and lesbian couples in therapy: Homophobia, relational ambiguity, and social support. In A Gurman & N. Jacobson (Eds.), *Clinical handbook of couple therapy* (3rd ed.) pp. 546-568). New York: Guilford Press.

Greenan, D. & Tunnell, G. (2002). *Couple therapy with gay men.* New York: Guilford Press.

Mason, M. (1991). Family therapy as the emerging context for sex therapy. In A. Gurman & D. Kniskern (Eds.), *Handbook of family therapy: Volume II.* (pp. 479-507). New York: Bruner/Mazel.

Ritter, K. & Terndrup, A. (2002). *Handbook of affirmative psychotherapy with lesbians and gay men.* New York: The Guilford Press.

Slakter, E. (Ed.) (1987). *Countertransference: A comprehensive view of those reactions of the therapist to the patient that may help or hinder treatment.* New York: Jason Aronson Press.

Resolving the Curious Paradox
of the (A)Sexual Lesbian

Marny Hall

SUMMARY. Lesbians' erotic lives have been bracketed by opposing sexual narratives. According to a variety of experts, sex between two women is an unnatural and unlikely event. Data from a number of other sources suggest that lesbian sex is both frequent and ecstatic. For many long term partners, these polarized narratives serve as filters, screening out a myriad of middle ground practices and scenarios. Because more subtle possibilities are invisible or discounted, couple's only alternative–after the passionate courtship phase of the relationship has ended– is lesbian bed death. In such cases, renewed erotic contact depends on the restoration of the erased sexual middle-ground. This paper focuses on the strategies clinicians can use to neutralize the hegemonic either/or lesbian sexual narratives and expand their client's erotic repertoires. *[Article copies available for a fee from The Haworth Document Delivery Service: 1-800-HAWORTH. E-mail address: <docdelivery@haworthpress.com> Website: <http://www.HaworthPress.com> © 2004 by The Haworth Press, Inc. All rights reserved.]*

KEYWORDS. Lesbian, lesbian sex, lesbian partnerships, lesbian couples, sex therapy, narrative therapy, lesbian bed death

Marny Hall, PhD, LCSW, is a psychotherapist in private practice (E-mail: Marny hall@aol.com).

[Haworth co-indexing entry note]: "Resolving the Curious Paradox of the (A)Sexual Lesbian." Hall, Marny. Co-published simultaneously in *Journal of Couple & Relationship Therapy* (The Haworth Press) Vol. 3, No. 2/3, 2004, pp. 75-83; and: *Relationship Therapy with Same-Sex Couples* (ed: Jerry J. Bigner, and Joseph L. Wetchler) The Haworth Press. Inc., 2004, pp. 75-83. Single or multiple copies of this article are available for a fee from The Haworth Document Delivery Service [1-800-HAWORTH, 9:00 a.m. - 5:00 p.m. (EST). E-mail address: docdelivery@haworthpress.com].

75

Lesbians have always been trapped in a paradox. According to a range of experts, beginning with medieval judges and continuing to present-day researchers, sex between two women is a highly improbable event. Just as puzzling is an opposing construct: a second group of theorists posits "sexually perverse" women (Krafft-Ebing, 1965, p. 262) as being s a l a c i o u s to their very cores–oversexed, prurient, insatiable.

The more chaste of the two viewpoints often prevailed in pre-twentieth century courts. In a classic Victorian case, two headmistresses of a Scottish boarding school, caught *in flagrante delicto* by a student, were accused of indecent acts. Subsequently, the headmistresses sued the student's family for damages and won. According to the presiding judges, the alleged crime did not exist. Two women, they ruled, "could not copulate without penetration of the female–any more than murder could be committed by hocus-pocus" (Faderman, 1981, p. 149).

The opposing perspective, featuring the "predisposed female–tainted with 'hypersexual character'" (Krafft-Ebing, 1965, p. 263) was championed by nineteenth and twentieth century physicians and sexologists. Treatments prescribed by these specialists for perversion and erotomania included hypnosis, hydrotherapy, chemotherapy, and surgery. Lobotomies were performed as late as 1951 (Katz, 1976, p. 129).

Although tempted to congratulate ourselves on the psychosexual distance traveled since those unenlightened times, closer examination suggests self-congratulations may be premature.

TWENTY-FIRST CENTURY POSTSCRIPT: THE PARADOX OF THE (A)SEXUAL LESBIAN REDUX

Today, most sex therapists consider Victorian and early twentieth century sexual perspectives as quaint as gaslights and corsets. We all know that lesbians exist, that sex between women is not due to "constitutional hypersexuality" or "gross sensuality" (Krafft-Ebing, 1965, p. 263). Despite our sophistication in such matters, the paradoxical (a)sexual lesbian has been resuscitated in the late twentieth century, infused with new life by a handful of social science researchers.

Among this group of well-meaning researchers were William Masters and Virginia Johnson. Influenced by feminism and later by gay liberation, the pioneering team set out to democratize sexuality. According to their laboratory findings, men and women, gays and straights all cycled through the same four stages of sexual response. "[T]here are no physiologic norms clearly distinguishing homosexual and heterosexual function," the author of the foreword to *Homosexuality in Perspective* claims. "[Therefore] the sexual dysfunctions of homosexuals can be treated as can those of heterosexuals" (Masters and Johnson, 1979, p. vii).

The triumph of the new paradigm–of genital functionalism over gender fundamentalism–seemed positive and progressive. The same-strokes-for-different-folks model mainstreamed lesbians and gays. Unfortunately, their new enfranchisement was conditional.

As long as they continued to be sexual, gays and lesbians would be allowed to hang out on the normal side of the newly constructed functional/dysfunctional faultline. But as newcomers to normality, they were on sexual probation. Whereas heterosexuals who stopped having sex remained "normal," gays and lesbians who abstained could be downgraded and reassigned to the stigmatized margins where they had traditionally resided.

The stakes were high when Blumstein and Schwartz published *American Couples* (1983). In the most exhaustive study of couples ever completed, survey questionnaires revealed that incidence of lesbian sex plunged after the two-year mark. Compared to their heterosexual and gay male counterparts, lesbian partners were the least "functional" of all.

Many explanations were proffered for the precipitous decline in the frequency of lesbian sex. Perhaps lesbians, socialized as women, were unaccustomed to initiating sex and, after passion had faded, retreated to earlier non-initiatory patterns. Perhaps female partners became so attuned to each other, so emotionally merged, that sex seemed redundant, and for some couples, even incestuous (Burch). Perhaps the survey used overly rigid, male-oriented criteria to tally lesbian sexual intimacy. Perhaps some combination of these reasons, or others, accounted for the results (Kotulski, 1996).

Even though the reliability of the lesbian data was challenged, the information was widely and quickly disseminated. This officially documented decline of the lesbian libido, dubbed Lesbian Bed Death by gay wags, became a frightening specter for couples. Thereafter they monitored themselves, waiting for its inevitable debut with a mixture of hopelessness and dread. Because small variations in sexual desire now occurred in the ominous framework of an epidemic, lesbian bed death–for many lesbian couples–became a self-fulfilling prophecy.

The functional paradigm that had seemed so gay-friendly at first merely succeeded in generating a newer, hipper faultline and another form of stigma. Models which do not continue to trap lesbians in the old familiar (a)sexual paradox are needed to treat lesbians with sexual complaints.

The LBD Remedy: Narrative Sex Therapy

Not long after Masters and Johnson had published *Human Sexual Response*, a group of social constructionists challenged their bedrock claims. According to this new wave of sex theorists, sex was provisional, fuzzy–constantly being pummeled and tweaked by macro and micro forces into novel shapes (Padgug, 1979). In traditional agrarian societies, for example, a procreative agenda shaped sexual narratives and practices. In contrast, the postmodern Western zeitgeist, with its emphasis on sexual pleasure, desire, and difference, has been shaped by contemporary capitalism (Altman, 2001, p. 55).

Lesbian narrative therapy (Hall, 1998, 2001, 2001) puts such malleability to good use. If therapists can help clients see around the edges of the either/or stories that have constrained and channeled lesbian sex, they can craft more subtle accounts.

These middle-ground narratives might include playful or planned sex dates, maybe-I'll-feel-like-it-after-we-start sex, let's-just-do-you sex, no-big-deal quickies, or friction-and-fantasy felicities, best summed up by the following exchange: "Did I make you come?" "No, Dear, but you were in the vicinity."

Lesbian clients are predisposed by their own coming-out experiences to find such an erotic smorgasbord congenial. In the process of declaring themselves queer, of (re)defining themselves as sex-and-gender renegades, most have already stumbled on the mutable nature of personal reality, on the benefits of rejecting psychological truisms about the "normal" course of female desire. In addition, narrative approach with lesbian clients has the advantage of being co-constructed–a give-and-take collaboration that gives clients both the permission and the means to write and rewrite their own sexual scripts. Finally, because narrative therapy is not a one-size-fits-all formula, it can mirror the ethnic, generational, and temperamental diversity of lesbians themselves.

NARRATIVE SEX THERAPY:
SIX INTERVENTIONS

There is a certain internal logic to the sequencing of the following interventions. The last stage, tune-ups, wouldn't precede the initial history taking. Nevertheless, therapists are not bound by the sequence and may find themselves circling around to revisit one or more of the interventions during the course of therapy.

Intervention #1:
History Taking: Honoring the Paradox

When they first come to sex therapy, most lesbian-couple clients have their own personalized, paradoxical tale to tell: a story of soul-stirring, even earth-moving sex, followed, in many cases, by the story of its gradual or abrupt cessation. Both parts of the story deserve their due. It is important for the therapist to solicit how, when, where, as well as the whys: couple's explanations for sexual infrequency. Accounts of the partner's erotic beginnings are equally important–particularly because initial passionate encounters often serve as benchmarks against which the couple measures subsequent sexual encounters.

As well as providing useful information about couple's sexual history and expectations, their accounts of passionate marathons may be the only way of certifying the legitimacy–in lieu of legal or familial recognition–of their unions. By attending closely to the romantic inception of the relationship, the therapist is bearing witness to a momentous event.

Intervention #2:
Loosening the Paradox/Rehabilitating the Middle Ground

Years before partners met, most were steeped in the paradoxical views of lesbian sexuality. Literature, films, friend's firsthand accounts, and qualitative research–full of depictions of lesbian's passionate encounters–leave their stamp on couples' own accounts. At the same time, if they have participated in the gay cultural scene, couples have been bombarded with lesbian bed death accounts from queer comedians, researchers, therapists, and journalists. Perhaps it is not surprising that these bipolar narratives bracket their experiences as a couple.

It is only logical that couples will try to escape the disappointing half of their contradictory love story by trying to reactivate their passionate prologue. Unfortunately, such attempts are doomed from the start–thwarted by the prevailing all-or-nothing versions of lesbian (a)sexuality. The two schematic narrative strands serve as filters, screening out scores of less dramatic, middle-ground stories about sex. For example, instead of being construed as a form of receptivity, a partner's if-I-don't-have-to-lift-a-finger brand of willingness will probably be dismissed as insufficiently reciprocal. A mutual masturbation session may also be filtered out–discounted as mechanical or unspontaneous. In other words, a single brand of acceptable sex almost guarantees a default to the only other story in the lesbian sex repertoire: lesbian bed death.

Sex therapists don't have the cultural wallop to neutralize the passionate sex narrative. It is simply too ubiquitous and compelling. As the sex therapy expert, however, she can limit its power within her domain. When she is explaining what partners may expect from therapy, she can say something like, "The sex that inaugurated relationship sounds incredibly powerful. We can't replicate the circumstances that contributed to it. But we can develop other kinds of sex that will be just as bonding and much more reliable and sustaining in the long run." Chances are, the therapist will have to repeat the agenda of developing alternative narratives many times during the course of therapy.

Intervention #3:
Continuing to Resist the Pull of the All-or-Nothing Narrative

Most couples hope to rekindle the passion by coming to therapy. Upon hearing that such attempts are off limits, clients will protest. After all, the therapist is removing hope for a much-desired ecstatic encore. In the ultimate act of defiance, some couples return after the initial sessions with a shocking announcement: they have indeed achieved the impossible. After years of trying, they have had passionate sex. The therapist, if she is not a cultural outsider, may find herself cheering, secretly rooting for its permanent return. These are white-knuckle junctures–the moments when it takes determination and conviction to continue to protect the narrative space in which other, more subtle stories/practices may be cultivated. If couples do return with breathless tales of rekindled passion, the therapist can acknowledge them and move on by saying, "That's great–not only because you had such a fabulous time but because it's a reminder of how passionate sex can overshadow more subtle and reliable forms of sex." If the therapist can resist the powerful pull to the passionate narrative, many couples will begin a phase of mourning, of existential questioning about the meaning of life and love. In this stage, it is important for the therapist to protect couple's open-ended exploration of post-passionate unions.

Intervention #4:
Helping Each Partner Rescue
Her Individual Narrative from the Paradox

Subtle middle-ground sexual possibilities aren't all that has been erased by the all-or-nothing narrative. Also buried are certain details of partner's individual stories, e.g., fantasies, taboo desires, masturbation habits, and pieces of personal history that seem incongruent or inconsistent with the partner's current efforts to revive passion and avoid bed death. In some instances such disowned details, instead of being buried, have simply been disguised or distorted. They may appear as depression or hopelessness, or as yes/no battles about sex.

Declaring passion off limits during therapy makes it easier for partners to reclaim these jettisoned parts of their sexual preferences or histories. Say, for example, one partner has disavowed her polyamorous past because she associates it with substance abuse–the unstable period in her life before she became clean and sober and committed herself to her current partner. With support from the therapist, this partner's disappointment about the post-passionate sex now available to her can lead to memories of "the old days." Acknowledging their long-denied positive aspects can help the client reclaim the disowned but crucial parts of her history.

The partner of the ex-poly may find this part of her past particularly threatening. Perhaps the more monogamous partner has a history of losing girlfriends after their ardor cooled. Previously unmentionable fears that her formerly polyamorous partner may abandon her as well, that she may be alone again, can now be articulated and included in therapy.

Though on the surface they may have little to do with the development of new sexual practices, admissions of hidden vulnerabilities, and the reclaiming of abandoned and discredited experiences, are probably the most critical parts of sex therapy. Because these details do not fit tidily into any hegemonic togetherness narrative, their airing and acknowledgement can help both partners escape the tyranny of all-or-nothing.

During these painful, revelatory passages, it is important for the therapist to help partners voice disappointments and doubts, to tolerate differences in sexual patterns and preferences, and to cope with some degree of future uncertainty.

Intervention #5:
In Vivo Applications: Shifting the Paradigm

Before they can become reliable additions to partner's repertoires, new sex narratives have to be developed and practiced. The timing and pacing of homework assignments (the means by which this new framework is developed) is a delicate process. If therapists wait too long, partners may be reluctant to switch from talk to action. If, on the other hand, therapists assign homework before partners have processed their feelings about the loss of passion, or if homework is assigned in a rigidly lockstep manner, clients will find reasons not to do it. As a general rule, even the most conflicted couples can handle some sort of assignment by the third or fourth session.

The exercises shift the old paradigm in several ways. Instead of paying homage to passion, they emphasize willingness and warmth. A new, meandering form of playfulness replaces the previous passion orientation. Instead of reinforcing reciprocity and equity, the exercises also give permission for asymmetrical roles and passivity. And finally, regularly assigned time-outs for planned sex replace the old regime's unpredictable interruptions of daily life by impulsive, impossible-to-resist sex.

The selection of particular exercises that meet these objectives, their tailoring and pacing, will be entirely dependent on feedback from the clients. A progressive series of massage assignments is often a useful way to shift the sex narrative to more playful, less passion oriented forms of eroticism. Gradually, over a series of weeks, partners are instructed to shift from generalized, diffuse touching to more focused massaging of erotic zones, stopping frequently to get and give feedback. For some partners, erotic massage comes to comprise a reliable new sexual narrative. Plenty of couples, however, won't find the massage route congenial. When one or both partners object to massage assignments, it is important for the therapist to supply a series of alternative exercises. For example, the therapist can instruct one partner to simply lie passively, to become a "rag doll," while the active partner gently moves all her limbs (Stubbs, 1999, p. 206). Perhaps they can simply spoon and synchronize breathing for the duration of the exercise. Perhaps they can be assigned a placeholder exercise: a fill-in-the-blank time where partners can figure out preferred modes of intimacy together.

Sometimes partners will introduce their own form of erotic touching into the exercises. Sometimes it may be up to the therapist to suggest its introduction. For example, partners, comfortably clothed, can be instructed to lie side by side, facing up, heading in opposite directions. That is, one partner's head will be level with the other's feet and vice-versa. The therapist can suggest that, using the most convenient hand, each partner reach over and gently cup her partner's genitals. Remaining quietly in this position for a few minutes, each can tune in to any changes in sensation. Or they can be introduced to a wide range of stop and start touch exercises. For example, partner A can be instructed to massage partner B erotically until B signals she is beginning to feel aroused. A should then stop stroking B and hold her quietly. When B notices that she is no longer aroused, the stroking should resume. Partners should repeat this stop/start exercise several times. A regimen of such interruptions can help couples deemphasize orgasm and tune-in to subtle differences in levels of arousal.

During this homework regimen, most couples develop routines that work for them. One couple instituted regular mutual vibrator sessions. Another client, spoofing the therapist's claims about the benefits of routine, planned sex, reported that she had purchased a janitor's jumpsuit, worn it home, and initiated "maintenance" sex. Yet another couple realized that one partner's peak erotic time was midnight, the other's, sunrise. They settled on Sunday afternoon bedroom sex picnics complete with lox, bagels, and the *New York Times*.

These new narratives are both tentative and delicate. Consequently, the therapist celebrates them as the extraordinary counter-culture achievements they are.

Intervention #6:
Tune Ups

When partners report that they have begun to perform their new narratives with some regularity, the formal phase of therapy is officially over. Outside the framework of therapy, however, the passionate sex and its asexual twin story are still hegemonic. Consequently, couples may need to come in for periodic tune-ups. During these sessions, the therapist can explore doubts, and disappointments, and reinforce new repertoires.

Epilogue: The Therapist's Own Repertoire

Up until this point, the focus has been on the strategies necessary for changing couple's stories. To be effective with lesbian couples, however, therapists must shift their own favorite narrative. Instead of thinking of ourselves as astute clinicians, able by adroit interventions to restore couples to sexually healthy functioning, we must imagine that we are members of a subversive sort of escort service. If we can believe in ourselves as counter-cultural map makers and tour guides, we will be able to help lesbian couples relocate from the trompe-l'oeil horizon of Ecstatically Ever After to a shape-shifting zone of sustainable intimacy.

REFERENCES

Altman, D. (2001). *Global sex.* Chicago: University of Chicago Press.

Blumstein, P. & Schwartz, P. (1983). *American couples.* New York: William Morrow.

Faderman, L. (1981). *Surpassing the love of men.* New York: William Morrow.

Hall, M. (1998). *The lesbian love companion.* San Francisco: Harper Collins.

Hall, M. (2001) "Beyond ever after: Narrative therapy with lesbian couples" in Kleinplatz, P. (Ed.) *New directions in sex therapy: Innovations and alternatives.* Philadelphia: Brunner-Routledge.

Hall, M. (2001). Epilogue: The demiurge remaps the semi-urge. in Kaschak, E. & Tiefer, L. (Eds.) *A new view of women's sexual problems.* New York: The Haworth Press, Inc.

Katz, J. (1976). *Gay American History: Lesbians and gay men in the U.S.A.* New York: Thomas Y. Crowell.

Kotulski, D. (1996). The expression of love, sex, and intimacy in lesbian and heterosexual couples: A feminist inquiry. Dissertation, California School of Professional Psychology, Alameda, California.

Krafft-Ebing, R. (1965). *Psychopathia sexualis.* London: Staples Press.

Masters, W. & Johnson, V. (1979). *Homosexuality in perspective.* Boston: Little Brown.

Padgug, R. (1979). On conceptualizing sexuality in history. *Radical History Review,* 20.

Stubbs, K. (1999). *The essential tantra.* New York: Jeremy P. Tarcher/Putnam.

SPECIAL ISSUES
WITH SAME-SEX COUPLES

Working with Gay and Lesbian Parents

Jerry J. Bigner

SUMMARY. Therapists are likely to be working with more gay and lesbian parents as these individuals become ubiquitous in society. Queer parents and their families present unique clinical issues that distinguish them from other GLBT clients. Issues commonly expected to be encountered in working with gay and lesbian parents are discussed in this article. These issues are restricted to those commonly experienced by married or once married queer parents and their families since these comprise the majority usually seen by therapists. *[Article copies available for a fee from The Haworth Document Delivery Service: 1-800-HAWORTH. E-mail address: <docdelivery@haworthpress.com> Website: <http://www.Haworth Press.com> © 2004 by The Haworth Press, Inc. All rights reserved.]*

KEYWORDS. Gay parents, lesbian parents, homosexual parents, queer parents, queer families

Jerry J. Bigner, PhD, is Professor Emeritus, Department of Human Development and Family Studies, Colorado State University.

[Haworth co-indexing entry note]: "Working with Gay and Lesbian Parents." Bigner. Jerry J. Co-published simultaneously in *Journal of Couple & Relationship Therapy* (The Haworth Press) Vol. 3, No. 2/3, 2004, pp. 85-93; and: *Relationship Therapy with Same-Sex Couples* (ed: Jerry J. Bigner, and Joseph L. Wetchler) The Haworth Press, Inc., 2004, pp. 85-93. Single or multiple copies of this article are available for a fee from The Haworth Document Delivery Service [1-800-HAWORTH, 9:00 a.m. - 5:00 p.m. (EST). E-mail address: docdelivery@haworthpress.com].

http://www.haworthpress.com/web/JCRT
Digital Object Identifier: 10.1300/J398v03n02_09

The social phenomenon of gay and lesbian parenting is becoming less sensational as the notion as well as the individuals and their children have become more visible. Indeed, as one researcher has observed, there appears to be a so-called "baby boom" especially among many lesbian couples who now embrace parenthood as a lifestyle via adoption or artificial insemination of one or both partners (Patterson, 1994). Because of the increasing visibility of both gay fathers, lesbian mothers, and the stepfamilies that are formed as a result of parenthood, therapists can also expect more frequent encounters with these clientele in their practices. Queer parents and their families present unique clinical issues and situations that distinguish them from other GLBT clients. Although there is not an extensive literature as yet about these individuals and their families, it is apparent that queer parents experience a distinctive and more complex social-psychological environment than that of other individuals in the gay and lesbian communities. And because of the trail-blazing nature of these relatively new lifestyles, many will need assistance in a variety of therapeutic areas.

PREVALENCE OF GAY FATHERS AND LESBIAN MOTHERS

The majority of queer parents appear to have assumed this status from a past heterosexual relationship (Bigner, 2000). However, it is impossible to accurately account for or even estimate the number of married or once married gay men and lesbians in the United States. The United States Census Bureau does not inquire as to sexual orientation in surveys of the population and has only recently asked individuals to indicate if they are living in a same-sex household. Conservative estimates based on extrapolation of information from census figures suggests that there are possibly 1 million married or once married gay men and lesbians in the United States (Buxton, 1994; Laumann, Gagnon, Michael, & Michaels, 1994). Other estimates place the number of children (including those who are now adults) of married or once married gay men and lesbians at almost 2 million (Bell & Weinberg, 1978; Moser & Auerback, 1987; Saghir & Robins, 1973). If homosexuals constitute at least 2 percent of the American population, then these groups of gay fathers, lesbian mothers, and their children clearly constitute a minority within a minority in our culture.

THE IRONY OF GAY AND LESBIAN PARENTING

Many couple and relationship therapists are likely to have limited clinical training as well as experience with gay and lesbian parents and their children. The knowledge base about queer parenting is fairly limited as well in that studies did not appear systematically until the late 1970s and early 1980s (Buxton, 1999).

The etiology leading to parenthood differs for gay men and lesbians, although some elements of causation are common to both. There is no simple explanation for the phenomenon but rather a complex of reasons have been suggested (Barret & Robinson, 1990; Benkov, 1994; Bigner, 1996; Bigner & Bozett, 1989; Crespi, 2001; D'Augelli & Patterson, 1995; Glazer, 2001).

Reasons Held in Common

Adoption often is a common route to parenthood among both heterosexual and homosexual individuals and couples as an alternative to natural conceptive methods. This does not occur as commonly among gay and lesbian parents as other routes to parenthood. It is likely that the majority of gay fathers and a substantial number of lesbian mothers became parents while involved in a past heterosexual relationship (Bigner, 2000). While it cannot be documented empirically, clinical observation strongly supports the notion that both were strongly influenced to enter heterosexual relationships because of high levels of internalized homophobia. Many likely entered these relationships with the sincere desire to avoid the negative stigmas associated with homosexuality and even, perhaps, to overcome these desires. The charade of heterosexuality for most cannot be maintained indefinitely as basic sexual orientation needs become manifested, especially in the vicinity of mid-life transition experiences (Bigner, 1996). As these pressing identity issues are addressed, both gay men and lesbians disclose their homosexuality to spouses. Divorce becomes inevitable for most, and few marriages remain intact following disclosure (Buxton, 1994). In the process of attempting to participate in a heterosexual lifestyle, one or more children are produced by gay fathers and lesbian mothers. Following divorce, most gay men become non-custodial fathers with visitation privileges while holding joint custody parenting rights. Most lesbians typically assume sole or joint custody of their children.

These individuals are challenged following disclosure to establish a conflicting personal identity: gay father or lesbian mother (Bozett, 1981; D'Augelli & Patterson, 1995). The adjustment challenges can be difficult and problematic. Many gay fathers and lesbian mothers seek to replicate the kind of committed relationship they experienced or desired in their former heterosexual arrangement. Because these individuals differ from most gay men and lesbians in having a heterosexual involvement in their past as well as children in their history, they may experience discrimination and isolation from the larger GLBT community. However, as these individuals become more visible and numerable, they are likely to become more accepted and unremarkable.

THE UNIQUENESS OF MANY LESBIAN MOTHERS

Although some gay men do not become parents by the above described route, many lesbians become mothers by alternative routes than past heterosexual involvements. Two approaches are commonly observed among these lesbian mothers: adoption and artificial insemination by donor (Crespi, 2001; Nelson, 1999). While most therapists are knowledgeable about adoption procedures and how this impacts couples, it is likely that preparation is helpful in understanding the uniqueness of lesbian parenthood via medical reproductive technology.

Since most lesbian mothers, regardless of the avenue taken to achieve motherhood, hold full custody of children, the focus is perhaps sharper and more acute on parenting roles and how to make these function in a family setting that includes two same-sex adults. When the assumption of motherhood is made by such deliberate and careful decision-making that involves reproductive technology and a birth takes place, challenges arise relating to roles within this family system as to who will assume primary care giving as well as provider roles. For these individuals, parenthood involves a major developmental challenge in creating roles and family patterns in a new family form for which there has been no previous modeling from families of origin (Crespi, 2001).

Since the majority of queer parents appear to have assumed this role via past heterosexual relationships and because of space limitations here, readers are referred to other sources for a more in-depth discussion of the particular therapeutic needs of lesbian couples choosing parenthood via reproductive technology or adoption (Glazer & Drescher, 2001; Sullivan, 1999).

CLINICAL ISSUES
IN WORKING WITH GAY AND LESBIAN PARENTS

There are some clinical issues that may be expected in working with gay fathers, lesbian mothers, their partners, and children which are held in common. Other issues are unique to gay fathers, particularly those who are married or once married. Others still are unique to lesbian mothers who are married or once married while those of other lesbian couples who assume parenthood outside of traditional heterosexual channels are even more particular to their group. These will be discussed briefly for married or once married queer parents. These issues may serve as presenting problems or can motivate clients to seek assistance as they encounter many of the challenges in establishing queer stepfamilies.

Identity Development Issues

Both gay fathers and lesbian mothers who are recently divorced may be expected to grapple with a major developmental issue following disclosure to self, spouse, other family members, and others as they seek to establish a new personal identity. This new identity attempts to be congruent with both their status as a parent and as a member of the queer community. As such, it may appear to be an enigma at first glance. The contradiction in terms and image must be reconciled into a meaningful whole that allows the individual to be recognized within the heterosexual community as a queer person while being recognized within the GLBT communities as a parent (Bozett, 1981a,b). Therapists can assist clients with this process by encouraging them to seek allies in the heterosexual community who provide validation for the gay or lesbian aspect of their identity. Likewise, clients can be encouraged to seek allies in the queer communities who provide validation of the parent aspect of their identity. Bozett (1981a,b) refer to this process as *integrative sanctioning*, as individuals meld these two seemingly disparate identity aspects into a meaningful whole.

In line with these issues, therapists can expect to observe patterns of extreme stress and emotional depression when clients first enter therapy (Miller, 1987). Anxiety, guilt, anger, irritability, and other depressive symptoms are likely to be observed as well as a variety of physical disturbances that are stress-related. Guilt may manifest in terms of internalized homophobia, in having lived a past life that was marked by deception and lack of authenticity, of leaving children or a spouse who may be seen as innocent victims, and of an uncertain future ahead as a queer individual. Many gay fathers, for example, may succumb to their guilty feelings which can dominate and influence what appears in divorce contracts that are to their later detriment. Such feelings may even spill over into relationships with children that become reconfigured following the divorce as both gay fathers and lesbian mothers move into a new lifestyle and personal identity.

One of the most challenging clinical tasks is to assist queer parents with their disclosure issues, not only to the self but also to children, spouses, and other family of origin members. This inner truth about the self has been couched perhaps for many years in secrecy and even denial. For many, self-recognition and acceptance as being queer may be the longest and most difficult phase of coming out (Eichberg, 1990). Once penetrated, often with therapeutic help, the process of constructing a positive self-image is launched. Therapists may observe some clients expressing extreme ambivalence initially about homosexuality. Many may express the desire to remain closeted after these initial first attempts. Clients can be assisted in becoming desensitized to the myths and stigmas long associated with homosexuality through bibliotherapy, and participation in coming-out support groups which help individuals to reframe internalized homophobic and heterosexist attitudes that have been so influential in these client's lives. Then, when clients appear ready to proceed in disclosures to former or current spouses and other family of origin members, therapists may provide assistance and support in these endeavors. Some may even desire support in helping to end their marriages.

Parenting Issues

Clinically, queer parents usually do not require nor request assistance with parenting issues, except when former spouses call this into question in legal proceedings relating to divorce and custody of children. Clients (and former spouses) may need support from therapists in being reassured about the large consensus of research studies on queer parenting. These studies consistently find that sexual orientation is an irrelevant issue in parenting, especially in divorce and custody proceedings, and that children are not harmed by being raised by a queer parent (Barret & Robinson, 1990; Benkov, 1994; Glazer & Drescher, 2001; Laird & Green, 1996; Sullivan, 1999). Therapists also may be called upon to provide expert witness testimony on behalf of queer parents involved in custody disputes relating to their effectiveness as parents. Detailed guidelines for providing such testimony are provided by Bigner (1996).

Disclosure to children becomes of paramount importance in the progress toward self-acceptance for many queer parents. It is also an excruciating decision and act since many fear that children will reject, cease to love, or cut off contact with them following disclosure. Therapists can provide support and assistance in this by helping queer parents understand that disclosure helps rather than hinders the queer parent-child relationship (Bigner, 1996). Research also supports this notion with findings indicating that disclosure validates the queer parent as being authentic and trustworthy by sharing rather than hiding this information from children (Miller, 1987). Additionally, therapists can refer clients, especially those who are unsure about logistics and timing of disclosure to children, to some general guidelines (Bigner & Bozett, 1989).

Developing Intimate Relationships

Gay fathers may experience a different path in developing intimate relationships from lesbian mothers. Both often desire a close, loving relationship with a same-sex partner, and many experience adult intimacy of this nature truly for the first time in their lives. Many queer parents will benefit from coaching in learning skills for dating same-sex partners, dealing with the intensity of romantic feelings, safer sex practices, and completing the process of becoming emotionally divorced from former spouses.

The situation for many newly emergent queer parents can be likened to that experienced by a young adolescent just testing the waters of intimate relationships. A therapist can act as a voice of reason as well as a coach or mentor for clients who are exploring the intricacies of gay culture for the first time. Clients need to be encouraged to explore and to grow from the experiences of romantic liaisons with same-sex partners.

While support and encouragement are being offered in these domains, it is also important to help clients to address the loss of the former heterosexual relationship and all that this involved. Queer parents are not immune from deal- ing with the emotional aspects of divorce and can profit from guidance in healing from the loss of the relationship with their former spouse. At this point, it may be helpful for both the queer parent and their former spouse to participate in joint sessions with the therapist so that both may work on bring- ing closure so that their separate lives can be moved forward.

Boundary Issues

A long-term committed relationship with a same-sex life partner forms the foundation of queer stepfamilies. These families are unique in the GLBT com- munities since children are involved, at least on a part-time basis for many gay male stepfamilies.

Issues that may be encountered in the formation and functioning of these stepfamilies often relate to boundary issues. For example, a common com- plaint of many gay men who become involved with a gay father relates to the father's past heterosexual relationship. Many feel that these fathers tend to im- pose a template as well as the manner of relating to the new partner based on what was experienced in the father's past heterosexual relationship. There are resentments of being treated like a wife might be. This often comes as some surprise to the gay father who is usually unaware of these dynamics.

Other boundary issues relate to the tendency for queer parent couples to iso- late themselves from the larger GLBT communities, their families of origin, and other social support networks. This is particularly a problem among some lesbian stepfamilies in that sexual orientation of the adults is likely to be treated as a family secret. This is due to the fear of losing custody of children if such information became public in some settings.

Another major aspect of boundary issues relates to relationships and inter- actions with ex-spouses and ex-in-laws. These relationships become modified following divorce and can have significant influences on the intimate relation- ships and interactions in newly formed queer stepfamilies. Readers are re- ferred to other sources for a more in-depth discussion of these issues, and especially to that appearing in this special volume.

Gender and Family Role Issues

Queer families have the advantage of redefining and reinventing the no- tions of family and parents because of their renegade positions involving gen- der (Benkov, 1994; Weinstein, 2001). Queer parents have greater latitude to explore and expand interpretations of what meaning to assign to parenting and other family roles since they are freed of gender influences as found in hetero- sexual families. Because gender is not relied upon in queer stepfamilies to de- termine who does what and how in childrearing and other family activities, there may be a greater opportunity to focus on and organize androgynous aspects in roles and responsibilities. Such arrangements are likely to call for negotiation that can be facilitated by the therapist.

CONCLUSION

Gay fathers and lesbian mothers present a complex challenge for therapists to assist them in growing toward a healthy, positive self-image and lifestyle. In summary, therapists can expect a therapeutic course to follow these points:

- Addressing intrapsychic disturbances relating to coming-out issues
- Helping clients to resolve internalized homophobic issues and facilitating the coming out process to self, ex-spouses, and children
- Helping clients to achieve a healthy, new personal identity as a gay father or lesbian mother
- Directing and encouraging client's socialization into the new world of homosexuality
- Assisting clients in addressing intimate relationship issues
- Assisting clients to resolve developmental tasks of queer stepfamily formation and functioning

The compassion and support of a competent therapist to challenge as well as to facilitate these numerous developmental issues can have far-reaching consequences in the lives of queer parents, their partners, and their children.

REFERENCES

Barret, R. L., & Robinson, B. E. (1990). *Gay fathers.* Lexington, MA: Lexington Books.

Bell, A. P., & Weinberg, M. S. (1978). *Homosexualities: A study of diversity among men and women.* New York: Simon & Schuster.

Benkov, L. (1994). *Reinventing the family: The emerging story of lesbian and gay parents.* New York: Crown.

Bigner, J. J. (1996). Working with gay fathers: Developmental, postdivorce parenting, and therapeutic issues. In R-J. Green & J. Laird (Eds.), *Lesbians and gays in couples and families: A handbook for therapists* (pp. 370-403). San Francisco: Jossey-Bass.

Bigner, J. J. & Bozett, F. W. (1989). Parenting by gay fathers. *Marriage & Family Review, 14,* 115-176.

Bigner, J. J. (2000). Gay and lesbian families. In W. C. Nichols, M. A. Pace-Nichols, D. S. Becvar, & A. Y. Napier (Eds.), *Handbook of family therapy: Dynamics and therapeutic interventions* (pp. 279-298). New York: John Wiley.

Bozett, F. W. (1981a). Gay father: Evolution of the gay father identity. *American Journal of Orthopsychiatry, 51,* 552-559.

Bozett, F. W. (1981b). Gay fathers: Identity conflict resolution through integrative sanctioning. *Alternative Lifestyles, 4,* 90-107.

Buxton, A. P. (1994). *The other side of the closet: The coming-out crisis for straight spouses and families, revised and expanded.* New York: Wiley.

Buxton, A. P. (1999). The best interest of children of gay and lesbian parents. In R. M. Galatzer-Levy & L. Kraus (Eds.), *The scientific basis of child custody decisions* (pp. 319-356). New York: John Wiley.

Crespi, L. (2001). And baby makes three: A dynamic look at development and conflict in lesbian families. In D. F. Glazer & J. Drescher (Eds.), *Gay and lesbian parenting* (pp. 7-29). New York: The Haworth Press, Inc.

D'Augelli, A. R., & Patterson, C. J. (Eds.). (1995). *Lesbian, gay, and bisexual identities over the lifespan: Psychological perspectives.* New York: Oxford University Press.

Eichberg, R. (1990). *Coming out: An act of love.* New York: Viking Penguin.

Glazer, D. F. (2001). Lesbian motherhood: Restorative choice or developmental imperative? In D. F. Glazer & J. Drescher (Eds.), *Gay and lesbian parenting* (pp. 31-43). New York: The Haworth Press, Inc.

Laumann, E. O., Gagnon, J. H., Michael, R. T., & Michaels, S. (1994). *The social organization of sexuality: Sexual practices in the United States* (pp. 283-320). Chicago: University of Chicago Press.

Miller, B. (1987). Counseling gay husbands and fathers. In F. W. Bozett (Ed.), *Gay and lesbian parents* (pp. 175-187). New York: Praeger.

Moser, C., & Auerback, S. (1987). Groups for the wives of gay and bisexual men. *Social Work,* 321-325.

Nelson, F. (1999). Lesbian families: Achieving motherhood. *Journal of Gay & Lesbian Social Services, 10,* 27-46.

Patterson, C. J. (1994). Children of the lesbian baby boom: Behavioral adjustment, self-concepts, and sex-role identity. In B. Greene & G. M. Herek (Eds.), *Psychological perspectives on lesbian and gay issues* (pp. 156-175). Vol. 1. Thousand Oaks, CA: Sage Publications, Inc.

Saghir, M. T., & Robins, E. (1973). *Male and female homosexuality: A comprehensive investigation.* Baltimore: Williams & Wilkins.

Weinstein, D. (2001). It's a radical thing: A conversation with April Martin, PhD. In D. F. Glazer & J. Drescher (Eds.), *Gay and lesbian parenting* (pp. 63-74). New York: The Haworth Press, Inc.

Paths and Pitfalls:
How Heterosexual Spouses Cope
When Their Husbands or Wives Come Out

Amity Pierce Buxton

SUMMARY. In up to two million couples ever married, one spouse has disclosed or may disclose being gay, lesbian, or bisexual. An increasing number of spouses are coming out, yet the phenomenon remains little known. Disclosing spouses generally find supporting organizations, while their heterosexual spouses find little support or understanding of their issues. Isolated, most cope alone. Dealing with sexual rejection, the challenge to the marriage, and, if they have children, spouse/parent conflicts is followed by handling questions about their own identity, integrity, and belief system. This piece describes issues that heterosexual spouses typically face and stages through which they move from survival to reconfiguring their lives whether or not they stay married. Peer support helps this process that lasts several years or more. Knowledge about spouse's concerns assists therapists working with spouses to help them resolve potentially paralyzing pain, anger, grief, or fear. *[Article copies available for a fee from The Haworth Document Delivery Service: 1-800-HAWORTH. E-mail address: <docdelivery@haworthpress.com> Website: <http://www.HaworthPress.com> © 2004 by The Haworth Press, Inc. All rights reserved.]*

Amity Pierce Buxton, PhD, Executive Director, Straight Spouse Network, 8215 Terrace Drive, El Cerrito, CA 94530-3058.

[Haworth co-indexing entry note]: "Paths and Pitfalls: How Heterosexual Spouses Cope When Their Husbands or Wives Come Out." Buxton, Amity Pierce. Co-published simultaneously in *Journal of Couple & Relationship Therapy* (The Haworth Press) Vol. 3, No. 2/3, 2004, pp. 95-109; and: *Relationship Therapy with Same-Sex Couples* (ed: Jerry J. Bigner, and Joseph L. Wetchler) The Haworth Press, Inc., 2004, pp. 95-109. Single or multiple copies of this article are available for a fee from The Haworth Document Delivery Service [1-800-HAWORTH. 9:00 a.m. - 5:00 p.m. (EST). E-mail address: docdelivery@haworthpress.com].

KEYWORDS. Mixed-orientation marriages, straight spouses, married gay men, married bisexuals, married lesbians, coming out

Up to 2,000,000 gay, lesbian, or bisexual persons in the United States have ever been in heterosexual marriages. Some have come out; others will, and some may never disclose to their partners. Disclosures within marriage have multiplied in the decades since the 1969 Stonewall Inn uprising and occur across all ethnic, socio-economic, religious, occupational, or education level groups. However, the phenomenon is little known, and, if known, little understood. When people hear about a spouse's disclosure, attention typically focuses on that spouse. The heterosexual spouse is typically overlooked and his or her devastation ignored. Outsiders tend to respond with comments like, "Your husband came out? Well, let him be who he is and move on yourself," or, in the case of heterosexual husbands, "Why are you still moaning and groaning? Your wife left months ago."

Without factoring in the heterosexual spouse's experience, the post-disclosure work of couples can be unnecessarily hurtful and destructive. The sexual orientation of both spouses is interwoven into the fabric of the marriage. Addressing the heterosexual spouse's experience as well as that of the disclosing spouse lessens the pain of them both and makes the outcome more constructive for everyone.

Even as known instances of spouses' coming out have increased in the past decade, a lack of awareness and understanding of the crisis persists, due to the slim body of literature on the subject and the invisibility of couples struggling with post-disclosure problems. Without knowledge and visible evidence, families of origin, friends, colleagues, co-congregants, or counselors of such spouses cannot help them in relevant ways. Moreover, the dearth of information limits the degree to which couples can deal realistically with a disclosure.

Heterosexual spouses, in particular, have suffered from the lack of information and public awareness. Until recently, most have coped alone. In isolation, their reactions intensified and issues blurred. While organizations that support gay, lesbian, or bisexual spouses increased in number since Stonewall, few have been available for spouses whose partners come out. As the Straight Spouse Network developed its support services over the past ten years, more and more heterosexual spouses have come out of their closets, amazed that they are not alone.

To fill the gap in the literature and increase public understanding, I have been gathering and disseminating information on the subject since 1986. At that time, there were some studies or trade books on married gay men and divorced lesbians, but few on heterosexual wives or mixed-orientation couples. Nothing was written about husbands whose wives had come out (Buxton, 2000).

To date, over 7,000 wives and husbands, gay, lesbian, bisexual, and heterosexual, have shared feelings, concerns, and coping strategies through consulting, interviews, correspondence, participation in private Internet lists, support groups, and regional gatherings; and conducting workshops and lectures. Several hundred children added their views. These self-reports form the basis of *The Other Side of the Closet: The Coming-Out Crisis for Straight Spouses* (Buxton, 1991); its expanded revision with more examples of spouses in bisexual-heterosexual marriages and children (Buxton, 1994); reports on couples who remained married after the husband (Buxton, 2001) or wife (Buxton, 2003) came out; and children's issues (Buxton, 2000).

Out of the diversity of paths that heterosexual spouses took to cope with their partner's disclosed sexual orientation, common issues and a typical sequence of dealing with them emerged. Most important, my sharing of these findings with spouses in such marriages lowered levels of fear, anger and pain for spouses and their partners. They were better able to withstand outside pressures to resolve issues quickly or to make decisions, such as divorce, based on faulty assumptions, misperceptions, or incomplete information. Many built bridges of understanding with their partners and made more considered decisions about their marriage and family.

Confirmed and honed through continued study and validated by other reports or biographies of heterosexual spouses in non-clinical settings (Atwood, 1995; Auerback & Moser, 1989; Brodsky, 2002; Deabill, 1987; Gochros, 1989; Gray, 2001; Hays & Samuels, 1988; Hill, 1987; Kohn & Matson, 1980; Latham & White, 1978; Maddox, 1982; Malone, 1980; Nahos & Turley, 1979; Nicolson, 1973; Pearson, 1989; Rogak, 1999; Schneider & Schneider, 1991; Whitehead, 1997; White, 1994; Whitney, 1990), key issues and stages of heterosexual spouses' journeys are ready to be shared more widely. What better audience than readers of this piece? Below, I briefly describe major issues and the progression of spouse's coping from initial trauma to some level of transformation.

First, several caveats. Coming out within a marriage is not an isolated event, but a family matter. Spouse's reactions, dilemmas, and decisions are affected by their individual personalities, the quality of the couple's relationship and habits of interacting, parenting and family activities, moral, value systems, and daily tasks and crises. Second, post-disclosure work occurs within multiple contexts of family and families of origin, socio-political and ethnic/cultural community groups, workplace, and faith community, each with its assumptions and pressures vis-à-vis homosexuality, bisexuality, and marriage. Third, presenting a process in terms of "stages" is done for clarity's sake. The heterosexual spouse's work is not a linear progression but proceeds on an uneven course, marked by overlappings, recurrences, and regressions of feelings and behaviors as he or she processes and reprocesses the disclosure in the light of new information, insights, or experience.

COMMON ISSUES

When heterosexual wives or husbands find out their spouses are gay, lesbian, or bisexual, most feel as if the world was ripped out from under them. Even those who suspected their spouses were homosexual or bisexual find the truth devastating. One wife comparing her life to a kaleidoscope said that the sudden appearance of the gay factor in the mix made it seem as if an unseen hand had shaken the pieces. The unfamiliar pattern was unsettling.

Devastation takes many forms, from thirty-year-old Sophia's freezing into inaction after she discovered her husband's e-mail correspondence to set up rendezvous with gay men; to forty-year-old Lou's planning suicide after learning his wife was having a relationship with her co-worker; to a sixty-year-old wife's curling up naked in a fetal position in her bed for three days when she found out her missionary husband had been having affairs.

In the first months, shock and disbelief overshadow underlying issues. Spouses who feel relieved to find an explanation for difficulties in the marriage or lovemaking are often too dazed by the truth to discern implications of the disclosure. For us to comprehend spouses' experience, however, it is critical to look at the issues that spouses eventually discern. Their realization of these concerns, one by one, marks the stages of their coping.

Concerns that confound heterosexual spouses relate to the same areas as issues that troubled their gay, lesbian, or bisexual partners as they came out to themselves: sexuality, marriage, children, identity, integrity, and belief system. (Note: Their children's problems, too, lie in the same areas.) However, the heterosexual spouse's perspective differs in most respects from that of their disclosing partners. The coming out makes their heterosexual orientation an issue in relation to the marriage, but it is not deemed ill, damned, or dangerous. They do not have to decide how to live in order to be true to a sexual orientation that differs from the norm. Even though they can see and feel their partner's struggle, they have no way of knowing what it is like to be gay, lesbian, or bisexual. At the same time, like their partners at the start of their coming out struggle, most heterosexual spouses begin theirs with the binary mindset that divides people into gay or straight and the false assumption that gay people do not marry or have children. They also share the social stigma attached to their partners by virtue of being married to them.

Heterosexual spouses become aware of key problem areas roughly in the order in which they are presented below. The timetable of addressing them varies from spouse to spouse, depending upon circumstances of the disclosure and subsequent events. If the partner simply acknowledges a same-sex attraction, the heterosexual spouse deals with issues as they come up. However, if a husband leaves a note by his wife's coffee cup announcing that he is gay and leaving, or a heterosexual husband comes upon a love letter from his wife to one of her female co-workers, or the disclosing spouse says he or she has had clandestine affairs or has a lover, or an AIDS diagnosis "outs" a husband–in those cases, issues arise quickly. No matter how fast spouses become aware of major problems, resolving them typically takes three or more years.

The first issues of which spouses become aware through day-to-day experiences relate to their sexuality, marriage, and children.

Sexuality

When a spouse says he or she is attracted to the same gender, the straight spouse feels rejected as a man or woman. Wives often feel they were not feminine enough to hold their husband's attention. Many husbands feel they were not enough of a man to have kept their wives from falling for a woman. Spouses often blame themselves as being sexually inadequate. Some fear that their sexuality may be damaged forever. Others feel shortchanged or dysfunctional. Wives whose husbands had or have extramarital sex fear they have contracted sexually transmitted diseases, including HIV.

Marriage

The disclosure prompts questions about the nature of marriage *per se* and the future of the couple's particular marriage. Spouses ponder whether or not a mixed-orientation marriage falls within the parameters of a traditional marriage and its monogamy and fidelity cornerstones. Regarding their own marriage, many spouses see the disclosure as a threat or death knell because of the betrayal or difference in sexual orientation. Others view the disclosure as a challenge to redefine the relationship so that it endures.

About a third of known couples break up at once, because the disclosing spouse has a lover or wants to live a gay life; or the heterosexual spouse no longer trusts the partner, does not want to live with someone who cheated or who the spouse believes to be immoral, or fears exposure to AIDS. Another third stay together for a year or two to sort out individual needs, wants, and values, reassess the relationship, and consider effects on their children. The remaining third commit themselves to trying to figure out how to make their marriages last.

Three years seems to be a turning point for whether or not a couple stays together. Among spouses who stay together either to assess their marriage or redefine its parameters, those who cling to the marriage-as-it-was find it harder to keep their marriage alive than do those who focus on their relationship. The latter take into account the kind of person each is, the quality of their relationship and patterns of interacting, and their individual strengths and weaknesses. Based on these factors, they redefine their marriages. New arrangements are generally of two types: variations on an open marriage for one or both spouses, with the couple's relationship primary; or a monogamous marriage with or without lovemaking within the marriage, and with or without the disclosing partner's having non-sexual same-gender friendships outside the marriage.

Creating the arrangement that best suits the couple takes a long time and creates a deep bond. Spouses who decide they cannot stay married nevertheless value their bond and it lasts beyond the divorce.

Compared to marriages of heterosexual and either gay or lesbian spouses, more bisexual-heterosexual couples seem to stay together longer inasmuch as both spouses are sexually attracted and pleasured by each other. More gay-heterosexual couples seem to continue their marriages longer than do lesbian-heterosexual couples; however, from my research, the number of couples still together after the wives came out appears to be higher than previously assumed. No matter which orientation, spouses in mixed orientation marriages often feel pressure to divorce from members of the gay community, who think marriage denies the gay or lesbian spouse's homosexuality, and from the straight community, who think marriage should be monogamous and/or homosexuality is immoral.

Children

Spouses with children worry about the impact of the partner's revealed sexual orientation on their children. An early concern is whether or not to tell the children about the disclosing parent and how to help them cope with antigay attitudes and behaviors in their neighborhood, school, or faith community. In most cases, the children are eventually told (or they find out), by either the parent who came out or both parents. Children react differently according to their age and stage of development and their individual personalities. Preschoolers sense tension, anger, and pain in the post-disclosure household. School age children generally feel embarrassed to have a parent with an unconventional identity, about whom classmates harbor stereotypical and derogatory assumptions or make anti-gay comments. Teenagers, especially those in middle school, do not want to be "different" or to keep their parent's sexual orientation a secret. If parents separate and divorce, as the majority do, the gay factor exacerbates concerns that are typical for any child of divorce: a division of loyalties to the parents, separation trauma regarding the non-custodial parent, and fear of abandonment by the custodial parent.

It is difficult for parents to watch their children hurt and hide, but children welcome their support, factual information, and guidance in dealing with teasing or rejection. The straight parent often serves as the model for the children's reactions. No matter how grievous the children's embarrassment, anger, or confusion, their love for the disclosing parent does not diminish. In the long term, none of the children's difficulties seem to have detrimental effects,

Parental concerns continue alongside spousal concerns about the marriage and their sexuality for a number of years. Internal crises of identity, integrity, and belief system become apparent in the second year after disclosure.

Identity

While the disclosing partners have found their true identity, heterosexual spouses feel that nothing is left inside them by which to identify themselves or to measure what they need, want or value. Tina, for example, whose husband came out shortly before the Oklahoma City bombing, felt like the news photo of the bombed-out Federal Building that appeared on every front page: walls torn open and interior wiring hanging loose. As family and friends ignore or minimize the spouse's agony, they begin to feel worthless.

Integrity

Most spouses feel that their moral compass was shattered by the partner's perceived deception and the disclosure that they are married to someone whom some people judge as evil and damned. They are no longer certain what is true or false, right or wrong. Deception by the partner, minor or grave, bothers most spouses more than the partner's being gay, lesbian, or bisexual. Spouses feel duped no matter what degree of self-denial, hiding, or lying by their partners or how much of a surprise it was to the partners themselves or how short a time lapsed between the partner's coming out to themselves and telling their spouses. Some, sensing they were living someone else's lie, worry that the entire marriage was a charade. Feeling betrayed, most lose trust in everyone's word and their own judgment.

The closet itself raises questions, especially for spouses who are asked not tell others about the disclosure. Many find themselves lying for the fist time. Spouses who tell others about their partners are tainted by the same social stigma or criticized for not knowing they were married to a gay, lesbian, or bisexual partner, wanting to stay married or, in the case of divorce, staying friends with their partners or continuing family activities.

Finally, the partner's homosexuality or bisexuality, and in some cases, same-sex behavior, become an issue for many, especially any who think that orientation and behavior are immoral.

Belief System

Disclosure by a partner shatters the picture the spouse had of gender, marriage, and life. Their belief system in pieces, spouses finds little meaning left in their lives and no purpose for which to reconfigure their view of life. Spouses struggle to explain their partner's changed orientation and their own suffering. Uncertainty about the future creates a sense of hopelessness.

WORKING THROUGH THE ISSUES

To work through these issues, heterosexual spouses typically move through seven stages. The goal is achieving a healthy sexuality, a positive working relationship with their partners, responsible parenting, a sense of individual authenticity, trust in themselves and others, and hope for their futures. At first glance, the stages resemble those described by Kübler-Ross in respect to processing someone's death. However, in the post-disclosure situation, the disclosing partner continues to be present and his or her newly revealed sexual orientation continues to impact the heterosexual spouse. Bargaining is between the spouses.

Each issue is freighted with intense feelings that can help or hinder a spouse's progress. In their initial shock, most spouses cannot pinpoint their emotions. Feelings arise only as they become aware of each issue. The most intense are hurt, anger, fear, and grief. Resolving the issues and managing the accompanying emotions usually takes three to six years . . .

Stage One: Disorientation/Disbelief

When their partners come out, spouses often think they are in someone else's drama or a nightmare from which they will awaken momentarily. Shock, disbelief, and denial predominate. Some feel relief from finding out the probable cause for sex-related problems in the marriage or recent changes in the partner.

Surges of anger over sexuality issues arise, but spouses are primarily confused about the disconnect between the disclosure and their past. Inability to grasp the facts keeps most spouses from moving quickly to the next stage. Continued denial often leads to stagnation, where spouses lose energy or will to deal with the truth. One such spouse, in his mid-twenties, whose wife came out and took their children to an Indian Reservation, fled by Greyhound to remote Rocky Mountain towns, one after another, finding work and staying just until he started thinking about what he was trying to escape. After five such stops, he ended up in a psychiatric hospital on suicide watch. There, he put his trauma into words for the first time in a poem entitled "Scream."

Stage Two: Facing and Acknowledging Reality

Day-to-day living or interacting with their husbands or wives brings spouses face to face with the new factors in their lives: the partner's sexual orientation, their own pain, and changes (in the partner, the couple's relationship, the heterosexual spouse, and the children). To look candidly at these factors requires courage, because doing so will prove the end of the life the spouses knew.

For most spouses, their partner's disclosed orientation seems to negate the basis of the marriage and causes embarrassment because of social stigma attached to it. This change makes some spouses question their own sexuality and their image of themselves as a man or a woman. Some blame themselves for the partner's "turning gay."

Looking at their pain from the disclosure, many discover emotional and mental wounds they fear will never heal or will leave lasting scars. If their partners minimize their hurt or blame them for being upset, they feel doubly confused. Wives who seek testing to find out if they are infected with HIV feel that their privacy has been invaded.

Changes in the partner are everywhere–his or her happiness at being liberated, different clothes or hairstyle, and/or new gay-related activities. The couple's conversations usually revolve around some aspect of the revealed orientation or gay-related events. Family activities are often modified to accommodate the partner's new schedule outside the home.

Regarding their children and their reactions to their parent's disclosure, spouses feel conflicted in their dual role as a parent and a spouse. They want to protect their children's bond with the parent who came out and also from difficulties the children might encounter outside the family because of having a gay parent. At the same time, spouses are hurting from the disclosure of the very person whose bond they want to protect and by the gay factor that they do not want to hurt their children.

Viewing the new situation without blinders and then acknowledging the facts therein evokes intense feelings, primarily hurt and anger. Spouses call it the roller coaster period when wishful thinking of the first stage is countered by negative feelings of this stage.

Spouses hurt mostly because the person they thought loved them caused their pain. For some, their pain and feelings as the "injured party" with no recourse intensify until they find themselves veering off the road on their way home or turning back to drinking or smoking. If the sense of being hurt is not overcome, spouses become stuck in the "victim" mode.

Anger erupts over their shortchanged or discontinued sexuality, the partner's self-absorption in his or her new life, or effects on the children. Anger sometimes turns into rage, which, for some spouses, causes heart attacks or leads to hatred of the partner. For others, jealousy of the partner's new happy life fuels their anger. Unresolved, anger turns to bitterness or vengeful outbursts against the partner and sometimes the gay community.

To work through their anger and hurt, many spouses, seek information to understand the partner's orientation, diagnose their pain, and assess the import of the changes through reading, workshops, activities in the gay community with their spouses, and sharing with peers. As they gain a realistic picture of their situation the next and harder step is to accept it.

Stage Three: Accepting

It takes most spouses months to realize that the new aspects of the partner and the marriage are irreversible, even if the couple stays married. Each factor that spouses accept represents a loss of something that was there before. Thus, the predominant feelings of this stage are anger that the changes occurred and grief over each loss.

Some spouses get angry with their partners over the disclosure-related changes. Many more vent their anger to peers, friends, or therapists, without targeting their partners, thereby releasing its negative energy. Not expressed or redirected, angry feelings stay in the resentment or vindictive mode.

Grief follows its own timetable, often helped by rituals that identify what was lost and its value to the spouse. Mourning is another place where spouses can become stuck, in a "pity poor me" mode. Unresolved grief leads to despair, depression, or suicidal thoughts or actions.

Full acceptance of their situation most often takes spouses two or more years after the disclosure. Though accepting, many feel anchorless, anxious about unknown consequences on their children and an uncertain future for themselves. If the facts are ignored or minimized, spouses remain in limbo with smoldering anger and lurking depression.

Stage Four: Letting Go

Once spouses accept their present reality, most let go of their picture of the past and rethink it in terms of the new information. In the process, most shed or diminish feelings of the earlier stages. Many utilize residual anger to take constructive action. They allow their grief to dissipate into sadness that is more wistful than wrenching, and value memories of the good parts of the marriage. They let their hurt dissolve. Some spouses make a deliberate act of forgiveness of the partner, themselves, society, or all factors involved in the coming out crisis. Not forced, forgiving brings peace of mind.

Spouses also rid themselves of unrealistic images, assumptions, and expectations about themselves, their partners, and their marriage. Self-blame, notions of romantic love, and wishful thinking disappear. Though many spouses feel empty and sad at this stage, most find a level of peace. The sense of emptiness usually prompts action to begin healing.

Stage Five: Healing

For months, spouses tend to focus so much on their partner that they forget themselves. As they let go of the past, most become acutely aware of themselves. Many are surprised at the extent of weight gain or loss, increased smoking or drinking, and lack of interest, drive, or joy. While they cannot change their partners or the mixed-orientation relationship, they can change themselves. Efforts to address their partner's needs can now be used to deal with questions about their own identity, integrity, and belief system.

"What about me?" signals the start of healing, which addresses identity and integrity issues. Feeling worthless, some spouses are reluctant to do something to help themselves. Slowly, they learn that self-care differs from selfishness or being self-centered. A first task is restoring an authentic identity in its physical, emotional, and cognitive dimensions. To improve their physical health, spouses begin to exercise and eat balanced, regular meals, behaviors that many forgot in the initial trauma. Many diminish or stop the drinking or smoking that helped dull their pain. To offset their fragile vulnerability, spouses regain emotional and psychological strength through interaction with friends and family members, and, most of all, peers, if they find a support group or discover Internet listservs for spouses. Many unearth buried interests, forgotten hopes, or neglected skills. A number discover or rediscover nature or the arts. In the cognitive realm, the challenge is to break down their dichotomous mindsets of gay versus straight, good and bad, and view the full spectrum of human behavior and sexuality. Slowly, many stop pinpointing the gay factor for anything wrong with the partner or the relationship.

Gradually, spouses see themselves as authentic persons, not dependent on any one else for happiness and responsible for their own well-being. Their self-image contains more strengths and skills than before and a candid view of weaknesses. With a sense of self worth, many feel joy in living and compassion for themselves and others. Their renewed wholeness makes them more present and helpful to their children.

Even self-assured spouses, however, feel betrayed by the partner's revelation, controlled by the "secret," and confronted by moral questions about their partner's orientation and in many cases, same-sex activities. Their partner's perceived deception provokes the most outrage, making most lose faith in their own judgment. Many spouses go in to their partner's closet because of the social stigma attached to homosexuality or their partner's request not to tell anyone. Some choose to keep the secret to protect their partners or children. Although some distinguish between "secrecy," which connotes shame, and "privacy" as a family matter, most feel uncomfortable lying. As these and other disclosure issues preoccupy their thoughts and they watch what they say and do because of the partner's disclosure, spouses begin to feel that they are no longer in control of the moral content of their lives. They feel helpless in deciding what to do. "What or whom can I trust?" triggers their realization that they are facing a crisis of integrity.

To discern what is true or false, right and wrong, for them, spouses lay out all their values to examine, select, and prioritize, add new ones, and put them together in a coherent form. As they work out their moral stance toward homosexuality, same-sex behavior, and the traditional marriage form, many encounter pressures one way or the other from friends or colleagues. Once their value system is in place, spouses make independent decisions with confidence, withstand criticism, and trust other people. Acting on their own truth lessens their anger and pain. For those who cannot restore integrity, confusion and fear persist.

Stage Six: Reconfiguring and Refocusing

Healed, many spouses still feel adrift and hopeless. Destruction of their former belief system lay at the core of their initial devastation. Now, with a clearer self-concept and moral compass, they become aware of a need for an updated belief system by which to put their situation in perspective and map their future. "Where can I find meaning?" triggers this stage.

Finding a purpose in life is a philosophical and, for some, a spiritual task. A number of spouses just "dream a new dream." Others take workshops in human development or recovery or read philosophical or religious books about suffering or ways to achieve inner peace. Still others seek alternative ways of coping, such as Native American faith in the Great Spirit or Eastern philosophies like Buddhist acceptance or the Taoist balance of opposites.

Gradually, spouses reconfigure a worldview that works for them. Most find the process exciting though scary in the face of an uncertain future. As their belief system becomes clearer, spouses gain hope and their fears lessen. Some wait for direction to come deus ex machina rather than discerning their own blueprint for transformation. Those who remain in a fearful mode, wondering about the future, become immobilized in depression or despair.

Stage Seven: Transforming

The final and continuing stage is transformation, when spouses move forward according to their reconfigured view of life, with or without their partners. This stage is the future-oriented, without pain from the present or anger from the past. Some spouses go back to school; others turn hobbies into businesses or become more productive at home or work; still others become more creative and responsive parents; and many deem their new faith in life the gift. Among spouses who are still married at this stage, some divorce because of the partner's homosexual orientation or same-sex behavior or the wish not to pursue an open marriage. Others separate by mutual agreement so that both spouses can be true to themselves and more at peace. Still others, educating themselves about sexual orientation and mixed-orientation marriages, broaden their value system and work to maintain the marriage. Some who do not condone homosexual behavior or open marriages work with their partners to minimize their homosexual attraction or behavior and create a monogamous or celibate marriage.

DISCUSSION:
SUPPORT AND SIGNIFICANCE

The route forged by spouses offers a road map for spouses newly facing their partner's coming out. Knowing that others have gone through the darkness and reached a lighter place offers a glimmer of hope. They see that pitfalls are not fatal, and that surprises may lurk around the corner as each stage is completed. Hopeless, they believe that they, too, may be able to find meaning in their lives again.

While only the individual spouse can resolve his or her issues, a spouse's work moves forward at a more natural pace if they are supported by a trusted friend and even more so, other spouses. With peer support and guided through potential danger spots by therapists, spouses more easily resolve questions and emotions that arise. If they cope alone, they more likely fall prey to unresolved anger, pain, grief, or fear. Unsupported, a number remain in denial or depression or strike out against his or her partners or former partners causing havoc for everyone.

Peers offer the most significant support, since they know what it is like to have a husband or wife come out. They listen, validate feelings, or share strategies; offer perspectives from their experience; and provide suggestions and resource information. They help each other to focus on their needs, wants, and values. They counsel one another that spouses cannot begin to heal until they face the situation and accept it. Support groups, face-to-face or on-line, offer a special kind of help. Listening or reading stories of other spouses at different stages demonstrates clearly that post-disclosure coping is a process that cannot be rushed.

Peers and therapists who have worked with spouse recognize emotional signals that point to the stage in which a spouse is coping. Intense pain and confusion mark early stages. Denial is stronger in the beginning but persists, since it is hard to accept painful reality. Grief is strongest as spouses realize their losses. Anger erupts most often in regard to issues about sexuality, identity, and integrity. Fear mounts as they accept reality and as transformation begins.

When intense emotions are not resolved, therapists are best equipped to help spouses work through them. While unresolved grief leads to despair and suicidal thoughts and fear can become terror, anger seems to be the trickiest and most destructive emotion. A spouse's anger is often misunderstood as a sign of homophobia, whereas most spouses become angry in reaction to feeling hurt, rejected sexually, deceived, and forced to change their life because of someone else.

Working through the issues provides spouses an array of strategies and insights that carry them in good stead in their relationship with their current spouse. By becoming clear about who they are and what they value, many develop skills of honest communication with their partner that will continue into future relationships for both of them, should they divorce. Most say that, through the coming-out experience, they grew wiser and more understanding about relationships and more accepting of differences in society, though they would not wish it on anyone.

REFERENCES

Atwood, A. H. (1998). *Husbands who love men: Deceit, disease, despair.* Providence, UT: MI Publications.

Auerback, S. & Moser, C. (1989). Groups for the wives of gays and bisexual men. *Social Work, July-August,* 321-325.

Bauman, R. (1986). *Gentleman from Maryland: The conscience of a gay conservative.* New York: William Morrow and Company.

Brodsky, R. M. (2001). *Jodi: The greatest love story ever told.* Lawrence, New York: Trebloom Publications.

Buxton, A.P. (1991). *The other side of the closet: The coming-out crisis for straight spouses.* Santa Monica: IBS Press.

Buxton, A.P. (1994). *The other side of the closet: The coming-out crisis for straight spouses and families.* New York: John Wiley & Sons.

Buxton, A.P. (1999). From hostile to helpful. In J. Wells (Ed.), *Home fronts: Controversies in nontraditional parenting* (pp. 201-212). Los Angeles: Alyson Press.

Buxton, A.P. (2000). The best interest of children of lesbian and gay parents. In R. Galatzer-Levy & L. Kraus (Eds.), *The scientific basis for custody decisions* (pp. 319-346). New York: John Wiley & Sons.

Buxton, A.P. (2001). Writing our own scripts. In B. Beemyn & E. Steinman (Eds.), *Bisexuality in the lives of men: Facts and fiction* (pp. 157-189). NY: Harrington Park Press.

Deabill, G. (1987). An investigation of sexual behaviors in mixed sexual orientation couples: Gay husbands and straight wives. (Unpublished doctoral dissertation, Institute for the Advanced Study of Human Sexuality, San Francisco.)

Gochros, J. S. (1985). Reactions to learning that their husbands are bisexual. In F. Klein & T. J. Wolf (Eds.), *Journal of Homosexuality 11(1/2),* 101-1148.

Gochros, J. S. (1989). *When husbands come out of the closet.* New York: Harrington Park Press.

Gray, C.G. (2001). *My husband is gay: A woman's guide to surviving the crisis.* Santa Cruz, CA: Crossing Press.

Hays, D. & Samuels, A. (1988). Heterosexual women's perceptions of their marriages to homosexual or bisexual men. *Journal of Homosexuality,* 17(3/4), 81-100.

Hill, I. (1987) *The bisexual spouse: Different dimensions in human sexuality.* McLean, VA: Barlina Books.

Maddox, M. (1982). *Married and gay: An intimate look at a different relationship.* New York: Harcourt Brace Jovanovich.

Malone, J. (1980). *Straight women/gay men: A special relationship.* New York: Dial Press.

Nahos, R. & Turley, M. (1979). *The new couple: Women and gay men.* New York: Seaview Books.

Nicolson, N. (1973). *Portrait of a marriage.* New York: Atheneum.

Pearson, C.L. (1989). *Good-bye, I love you.* New York: Jove.

Rogak, L. (1999). *Pretzel logic.* Grafton, NH: Williams Hill.

Schneider, J & Schneider, B. (1991). Gay and bisexual husbands. In J. Schneider & B. Schneider (Eds.), *Sex, lies, and forgiveness: Couples speaking out about sexual addiction* (pp. 183-222). Center City, MN: Hazelden Foundation.

White, M. (1994). *Stranger at the gate: To be gay and Christian in America.* New York: Simon-Schuster.

Whitehead, S. L. (1997). *The truth shall set you free: A memoir.* San Francisco: Harper San Francisco.

Whitney, C. (1990). *Uncommon lives: Gay men and straight women.* New York: Plume Books.

An Interpersonal
and Intercultural Embrace:
A Letter of Reflection
on My Gay Male Relational Connections

Eric Aoki

SUMMARY. Using Ono's (1997) "letter" format to share one's multiplicity of "voices," I discuss the negotiation of interpersonal and intercultural factors of a gay, transcontinental, HIV serodiscordant relational connection with my late partner and a multicultural relational connection with my current partner. In this letter, I work to open paths of inquiry and understanding of our connections by intersecting relational "differences" (e.g., ethnicity, nations of birth, social class, HIV status, and religion/spirituality) with relational "similarities" (e.g., attraction and love, age status, shared gay identity, shared languages, and educational privilege). Finally, I address our learned and practiced skills for sustaining relational healthiness. *[Article copies available for a fee from The Haworth Document Delivery Service: 1-800-HAWORTH. E-mail address: <docdelivery@haworthpress.com> Website: <http://www.HaworthPress.com> © 2004 by The Haworth Press, Inc. All rights reserved.]*

Eric Aoki is Assistant Professor, Department of Speech Communication at Colorado State University, 214 Willard Eddy Hall, Fort Collins, CO 80523-1783 (E-mail: Eric.Aoki@colostate.edu).

The author would like to thank Dr. Joseph L. Wetchler and Dr. Jerry J. Bigner for their insightful comments on an earlier draft of this essay.

[Haworth co-indexing entry note]: "An Interpersonal and Intercultural Embrace: A Letter of Reflection on My Gay Male Relational Connections." Aoki, Eric. Co-published simultaneously in *Journal of Couple & Relationship Therapy* (The Haworth Press) Vol. 3, No. 2/3, 2004, pp. 111-121; and: *Relationship Therapy with Same-Sex Couples* (ed: Jerry J. Bigner, and Joseph L. Wetchler) The Haworth Press, Inc., 2004, pp. 111-121. Single or multiple copies of this article are available for a fee from The Haworth Document Delivery Service [1-800-HAWORTH. 9:00 a.m. - 5:00 p.m. (EST). E-mail address: docdelivery@haworthpress.com].

KEYWORDS. Gay relationships, intercultural relationships, HIV serodiscordant relationships, ethnic studies

29 March 2003

To Whom It May Concern:[1]

Please allow me to begin this letter[2] by noting that my conception of "love" was joyfully practiced, challenged, and altered in my days with my late partner, Trevor,[3] and it continues to be lived out with my current day partner, Ryan. As a university professor, I, in addition to teaching intercultural communication, also teach interpersonal communication and the concept of love in its many forms (i.e., *ludis, pragma, eros, storge, mania* and *agape* to name a few) (Stewart & Logan, 1998).

In the four-plus years that Trevor and I lived "out" our relational life at a distance, from Fort Collins, Colorado and London, England, we negotiated an "open" relationship. We did this for reasons of pragmatic love. Trevor and I believed these reasons were not exclusively understood, but maybe more easily understood, if in fact, you are "loving" as individuals in a long-distance, transcontinental, intercultural relationship where both partners have busy career commitments (e.g., university professor and lawyer) and who also negotiate an HIV serodiscordant relational situation; Trevor and I were in a situation where he was HIV-positive and I am HIV-negative. In Sullivan (1998), an individual of HIV-positive status asserts, "I don't date HIV-negative guys anymore. They can be great people, but they just don't understand" (p. 74). Having experienced a HIV serodiscordant relational situation, I understand better this individual's comment regarding the challenges of partner empathy. Nonetheless, Trevor and I chose to remain connected. Hence, our relational connection[4] to each other was lived with a consciousness and commitment that had its share of interpersonal and intercultural challenges yet its own distinct beauty.

From the beginning, most family and friends supported our relational life, although it is fair to say that most did not envy or desire our relational set up and most did not fully understand the situation we faced and sometimes the decisions we made. In discussing challenges to intimacy between HIV serodiscordant partners, Palmer and Bor (2001) assert,

> As the couples became more used to living with an HIV-positive diagnosis and perceived it as less threatening to the relationship, so [sic] sexual behavior between partners began to "normalize." Other seropositive participants found they had little, if any, desire for sex after diagnosis, and this lack of libido continued to affect the sexual relationship with their partners well after an initial "settling down" period. Even if concerned about this, participants did not access services for help with these

sexual difficulties. The seronegative participant in these relationships had usually negotiated with his HIV-infected partner permission to have casual sexual relationships with other men. His partner's lowered sexual interest (possibly because of antiretroviral treatment or advancing illness) made this more possible. (p. 429)

Having framed the complexity of our relational situation, a situation that I would like to emphasize was challenging emotionally, physically, and practically, it is the case that Trevor and I, early on, negotiated allowances for me (seronegative) to continue to have intimate and respectful (not careless or casual) relations with other men. Trevor, by his preference, always knew about the men I was intimate with and these men always knew about Trevor and our relational status as HIV serodiscordant partners. In our situation, more specifically, Ryan became a part of our lives and continues to be my current partner; Trevor, however, did not have sexual or intimate relations outside of our immediate relational life.

Particularly in the early days of our connection, I was mostly scared of negotiating my life with Trevor, a man I was in love with and whom I also knew was HIV-positive. As Palmer and Bor (2001) state,

Rolland's (1994) work on the impact of illness on couple's relationships is seminal in understanding how HIV infection affects both the seronegative and seropositive partners and the psychosocial strain that results. . . . Rolland recognizes that couples need to be able to adapt the relationship to the changes illness may bring–on a continuing basis–as the disease progresses toward possible death. This is most evident in the importance of continuing to revise intimacy within the relationship to include (rather than try to exclude) illness and the threat of death. (p. 419)

So, Trevor and I consistently reevaluated our intimate life, internally, as his illness progressed. We also consistently assessed, externally, our connection with Ryan, letting him fully know Trevor's condition while also listening to Ryan's needs and perspective as well. Although there was a period of years when Ryan and I discontinued our sexual and companion-oriented relations (for the two years that Trevor and I were relationally monogamous), we continued to maintain our friendship with one another. Presently, Ryan, in the days since Trevor passed away, is once again the individual with whom I continue to share my life–emotionally, physically, spiritually and romantically. In our lives, this connection with one another involves a shared history of joy, passion, integrity, loss, compassion and honor in the expression of our love, a love that is quite different in feeling than any other love I have known in my life. Ryan has been fully present in the grieving and healing process since Trevor's passing, so our connection, presently, is a complex one.

With this complexity, Ryan and I realized then and we realize now that there exist individuals who hold a stigmatized perspective on our lives and the choices we have made. But, again, as men who love(d) in a complex matrix of situational variables, we consistently agree(d) to realize the strengths and beauty of our love.

My relational connection with both Trevor and Ryan, both of whom are distinctively complex in their own cultural backgrounds and identities, is the foundation of the sharing of love (again, in so many forms) in our lives. In explaining the love we share(d) with family, friends, my students, colleagues and even with a few therapists, after Trevor passed away, I realize retrospectively that it is difficult to capture the nuances of our love, generally, and more specifically with the many diverse conditions that we negotiated and continue to negotiate. Presently, in healing from loss, I cannot say that my efforts to remain in any type of sustained therapy has been anywhere near a noble effort. I am not proud of my record, for I have historically been a proponent of formal therapy, but I can only say that much of my grieving and healing thus far has been conducted with friends, family, and even acquaintances and strangers who have experienced somewhat similar situations of loss. I also direct much of my "voice" on "same-sex love" and "loss" into my artistic realms of painting and writing. These have been my mediums of expression (e.g., anger, sadness, joy, confusion) and healing for much of my life's personal and cultural challenges (e.g., racism, classism, homophobia, and relational loss).

With regard to my relational life and healing from loss, most of my friends and family have provided unconditional love and support, even when their attempts to understand our love have been challenged. I know that having support networks is a privileged position to occupy, for I have heard life stories about how the lack of social support can seriously affect the relational connection of partners–"gay," "straight," "interracial" and otherwise. Regardless, I also know that for reasons of my improved holistic health and for the love I share with my family, friends, and, more specifically, Ryan, I may need to seek additional counseling on these issues and concerns that often are not recognized, understood, favorably viewed, or supported. With regard to gay identity, specifically, I have learned in the thirty-four years of my life that often there exists the power of silence and an absence of support from society.

Although the life circumstances noted above provide some insight into our "personal-cultural" challenges and reflections, in the remaining pages, I address in greater detail the cultural complexities and benefits that are/were very much a part of my relational life with Trevor and Ryan. As gay men, where each partner is culturally at a distance (i.e., me, in Colorado; Trevor, in London; and Ryan, in California), diversely multicultural in ethnicities and nationalities (i.e., me, Mexican American & Japanese American; Trevor, British & Spanish; and Ryan, White American & Porteño–from Buenos Aires, Argentina), varied in social class histories (i.e., me, working-class U.S. American; Trevor, upper-class British; and Ryan, upper-class U.S. American), and diversely socialized in early day religious or spiritual influences (i.e., me, Catholic/Buddhist; Trevor, Agnostic; and Ryan, Catholic) sharing love added distinct challenge to our lives. This complexity also adds challenge to those individuals working to understand, from the outside, cultural differences and similarities in our intercultural, long distance, same-sex partner lives.

The experiences I share through my own case are not meant to speak for other's voices and lives. Rather, I share my situation to hopefully illuminate channels of inquiry and thought so that conversations on issues that potentially impact our lives as multicultural, Lesbian, Gay, Bisexual, and Transgender (LGBT) individuals may continue to be had. I hope to accomplish this goal with a "voice" that invites respect and a sense of integrity for an already socially stigmatized co-cultural group of society.

In our situation, it is important to note that all three of us held (and Ryan and I continue to hold) educational, cultural, social class, and male privilege in our lives. Nonetheless, negotiations regarding socio-cultural aspects of our relational life were of some challenge to us due to "difference," particularly in the early days. Martin and Nakayama (2000) state, "dissimilarity may account for the initial attraction, but these students talked about the importance of finding some similarity in their relationships that transcended the cultural differences" (p. 275). At the personal level, despite cultural difference and social stigmatization, we found common ground in being attracted to cultural difference, being multicultural in our identities, and sharing in love as gay men.

Early on, I remember negotiating differences between Trevor and I. Trevor was more reserved in his overall presentation of self while I have been in my lifetime, mostly, quite the opposite. As an international lawyer conducting business with U.S. American personnel on a routine basis, Trevor would tell me that I was still the most vocal and unreserved "American" he had ever met, hence, I did not fit his stereotypes of me as an "overly strategic American," a "quiet Asian" or even an "excessively closeted"[5] (Murray, 1996, p. 260) Latino. Additionally, Trevor had to get comfortable with "dating" someone who had tattoos on his body, for although he was "liberal" in politic and overall world view, he was quite "conservative" when it came to body art. Although Trevor knew tattoos were becoming increasingly present on people's bodies, his early day socialization in his British circles taught him that mostly "rough" individuals and individuals of the lower class had tattoos. On the other side of our cultural negotiations, I wrongly assumed that Trevor would be "British conservative" in being "out," for he had been liberally "out" in a supportive household since he was nineteen. Additionally, he found the comfort and privilege of being "out" at work and quite often in many other social contexts as well. I soon learned that Trevor's parents were more concerned with me "living at a distance" than being "Japanese American/Mexican American," "historically working class," or "gay." With all of these diverse factors of my identity that I typically was accustomed to having to negotiate, Trevor's parents did not hesitate once and took me in as their own "son." Even within my own "liberal and diverse" U.S. family, this negotiation of sexual orientation would be an accepting and loving one, yet not as smooth, for I had Mexican-Catholicism and some traditional Japanese influences to negotiate.

At the outset of our relational life, Trevor and I had to adapt to the accents and lingo that we each used from our "home" countries. These days I still use expressions like "going on holiday," "going to the loo," and "going bloody insane" that I picked up from Trevor. Also, both of us were proficient in various levels of Spanish language use. Trevor knew Mexican Spanish and Catalonian from Barcelona (his mother's heritage) and my Spanish was grounded in Californian and Mexican Spanish (my mother's heritage). To our benefit, when reasons of enhanced privacy were needed in public to discuss our relational life as "gay men," for reasons of "safety" and/or to avoid homophobic scrutiny, we could code-shift into our hodge-podge mix of Spanish. This shift did not guarantee privacy in full, but in some locations around the world, including in Colorado, we believed it gave us more freedom to speak freely about our romantic life. Currently, I also share this intercultural benefit with Ryan, as he speaks English, Spanish, and additionally, French. In fact, despite needing to speak predominantly English in my university and community life in Fort Collins, Ryan, in our personal lives, for the last six months, has spoken to me predominantly in Spanish.

With regard to our religious orientations, I grew up Catholic with some Buddhist influence and Trevor always identified as Agnostic. Although we both, in our adult lives, would avow to having spirituality in place, we had to work through subtle differences in the way we discussed and celebrated holidays like "Christmas," for Trevor did not celebrate it in the "Catholic," "U.S. American," or even "U.S. material" manner that I practiced and knew. Additionally, although I currently do not practice organized religion, Trevor still had to make room for the fact that I needed time to engage in some of my Catholic prayers at night (for ritual) as well as Buddhist meditations in the morning.

Likely, the most difficult challenge, HIV issue aside, is the cultural issue of being gay men. Because Trevor and I were often "open" with our love, in a simple gesture of holding hands in public, we received, often enough, under-the-breath, pejorative comments and unfriendly stares by individuals who actively disapproved of our relational life, even as complete strangers to our lives. Trevor and I traveled the world together extensively and in each new location, we always researched, without fail, where the "safe and friendly" areas were located, so we could be visible with our lives, if recommended at all. More often than not, people who were uncomfortable and disgusted by our relational connection would turn away or ignore our presence, but on occasion, people were cruel and direct. Despite Trevor's preference for privacy and his overall reserved manner, we chose, more often than not, to be public in order to help make more visible a socially oppressed and stigmatized identity. This negotiation of "being visible" or "choosing to not be visible" as gay men at any given moment or in any given context was quite a bit of work to attend to in our relational life. I am quite certain that individuals who hold the privilege to be visible in their relational lives without reservation or hesitation (I am speaking mostly of heterosexual privilege) do not fully comprehend how being "gay" publicly is in fact a cultural challenge that potentially changes and affects how and who you are in *both* your public and your personal life.

Socially, in my life, being gay has been the most difficult diversity identity to negotiate because of the invisibility and stigma factor. It is also an aspect of diversity that I have spent the least amount of "practice-time" with in various social contexts. Although I still experience negative incidents and feelings with regard to my ethnicity in public life (a visible identity feature), being gay has been the more challenging and at times overwhelming cultural variable to negotiate.

Personally, at another level of reflection, I have been internally conflicted by the visible ethnic difference of the men I have dated and who have been relational partners in my life. In the early days of my dating life in Fort Collins, the men that I met locally and even in Denver and Boulder were more often than not "White Americans." At that time I was struggling with why it seemed that who I was attracted to was more often than not "White" or "European." When I partnered up with my very first-boyfriend, the same Ryan of today, I was quite conscientious of the fact that he *is* and also looked "White," even though I also learned he was internationally multicultural and trilingual. Although I fell in love with Ryan because of his adorable personality, passion for politics and the environment, and shared interest in travel, he and I broke up amicably after eight months. The breakup was mostly due to my need to be visible and out in my life and his need at that time to be "closeted." Ryan's teaching career and his struggle with his religious roots of Catholicism posed serious concern to his desire and ability to be "out" at that time. Ultimately, the divide in our visibility/invisibility needs was too wide for us to continue, so we broke up.

Several months later, I met Trevor and he and I became increasingly more involved, romantically; At that point, Ryan remained present in my life as a friend. Martin and Nakayama (2000) state,

> What we know about gay relationships is often in contrast to the "model" of heterosexual relationships. Gay relationships may be intracultural or intercultural. Although there are many similarities between gay and straight relationships, they may differ in several areas: in the role of same-sex friendships, the role of cross-sex friendships, and in the relative importance of friendships. (p. 271)

With Trevor now as my primary relational partner, this did not mean disconnection from Ryan. Unlike situations in my past (when dating women) and with many of my heterosexual friends who would move from relationship to relationship and have no contact with (or could choose easily to lose contact with) their previous partner, I learned that I could no longer follow that model for reasons of community. As a gay man, leaving behind previous partners potentially meant limiting the notion of friendship and more importantly it meant cutting oneself off from the very population of people (sometimes a small network) who are often your strongest base of "identity" support. With my friends whom are "gay," I quickly learned that past lovers often became friends, support community, chosen "family," and even sometimes, like with Ryan, lovers again.

Like Ryan, Trevor too, looked visibly "White-American," even with his multi-cultural, British-Spanish heritage and trilingual fluencies. So, in the end, my heart simply loved whom I loved yet I would be remiss to not include that I struggled with the question, "Why am I not attracted to ethnic minority men of the United States, particularly when I, myself, am one?"

Several interlocutors in Wat (2002) discuss how historically, within the gay community, Asians often competed with other Asians for White men and how "Asians never like other Asians" (p. 71). One interlocutor of "Asian" background asserts, "Now that I look back on it, I think it was very racist in a sense. Asians were not attractive to me. My models were primarily Caucasian models" (p. 71). The same interlocutor also states, "You always talk to other people, but don't talk to gay Asians because they're family" (p. 71). In my own experience of dating and partnering up with Trevor and Ryan, I was at some level conflicted because of my questions regarding the "ethnic why?" and "why not?" of attraction.

Generally, I am able to see how my social context, networks, exposure to U.S. media, and my overall living situation influenced my attraction to the men I dated. I also realize that my initial non-attraction to U.S. ethnic minority men, specifically, was in many ways linked to the difficulty of viewing my typically "U.S. ethnic minority brothers" of society as someone to engage in romantic and sexual relations with in my life. These "ethnic minority brothers" often seemed too much like my own "brothers" and "father" in how we understood each other and connected in our ethnic social struggles. It may also be the case that it was easier, particularly early on, to connect romantically with a *man* of a distinctly different ethnic and cultural background than my own (in my case, two men with non-U.S. and mixed U.S. international backgrounds). So, early on in dating, it felt awkward to have to negotiate a romantic connection with someone who I had for many years of political life and advocacy in the U.S. viewed as more often than not, "ethnic brothers" with whom I "work and fight with" for reasons of social justice within the power systems of the United States–again, "ethnic brothers" felt too much like family.

In a different way, I made peace with my attraction to Ryan and Trevor. My relations with these two men are similar to the struggles and benefits faced by people like my own parents–the two people who have served as my relational role models through thirty-seven years of marriage. In the case of my parents, they negotiated the challenge of being ethnic minorities of the United States (i.e., my mother, Mexican American and my father, Japanese American) in an interracial marriage of the mid-1960s. Thus, my parents know the experience of *both* personal and social non-acceptance as a socially stigmatized, "interracial" couple. My relational connections with Ryan and Trevor brought forth much love; The connections also brought forth challenging thoughts of being connected, relationally, to systems of ethnic and class visibility and privilege that I had viewed culturally, at some level, as historically oppressive to my own life. Not that it mattered, but if people got past the gay relational connection, I could sometimes "hear" them saying, "you're dating a 'White' man" or the flip of this statement, even though this characterization had its inaccuracies too. Ultimately, the key was learning how to distinguish individual and cultural variables of our relational connection while also acknowledging the privileges, identity politics, and hard histories that came along with it.

As Trevor and I walked hand in hand, and now, as Ryan and I walk hand in hand, publicly, the stares we receive are usually relegated to our "gay" file of negative experiences. Ryan and I also know that the stares processing the visible interracial dimensions of who we are also compose the intersecting "race" file. If the stares go unspoken, which these days we prefer, it usually means less confrontation. We know that the stares can be complexly about people's homophobia, racist views, a mixture of both, acceptance, or even just plain curiosity when witnessing a display of our love for one another. Occasionally, we receive a nod and smile. For example, recently, Ryan and I received a compliment from a woman in Paris, a city that Ryan and I play out well in, who said to us, "seeing two boys kissing is very sexy." We looked at her and smiled.

In the end, with our love as our guide, I, along with both Trevor and Ryan, have practiced some of the basic teachings of "dialectics" to talk through our cultural foundations and experience. Martin and Nakayama (2000) put forth the cultural skills of thinking within "the entire relational sphere" to avoid stereotyping in intercultural relationships (pp. 272-273). Hence, in our intercultural, gay, relational life we have discussed the following intercultural dialectics: differences-similarities, cultural-individual, privilege-disadvantage, personal-contextual, static-dynamic, and history/past-present/future (Martin and Nakayama, 2000, pp. 273-275). Additionally, we have worked to get beyond the "cult of masculinity" by exploring intimacy; As Signorile (1997) offers, "Real intimacy requires hard work: It means being honest with others and ourselves. For some of us it means going into therapy, for others it means having the fortitude to be truthful with ourselves on our own" (p. 314). Trevor, Ryan, and I work(ed) to discuss "the trouble with normal" (Warner, 1999) and interrogate what "normal" as dictum meant and means for our lives. Specifically, we have examined the power discourses of "normal" and assessed the limitations it brings forth when living a life that typically is viewed outside of that constructed center. We have worked on all of these elements knowing that growth and progress (personally, relationally, and socio-culturally) are about strength of process and open communication.

Finally, in speaking of a diversely cultured life that I feel privileged to have lived thus far, and despite the personal and socio-cultural challenges that have been a part of it, I hope this "letter" provides, in some small way, a means to reflect on and embrace what living a life filled with love, compassion and integrity can be.

With Respect,

Eric

P.S. Should you want to check out some of the books I mentioned or get further clarification on items noted in this letter, what follows are the Notes and References.

NOTES

1. I address this "letter" to a faceless audience, yet an audience that holds "connection" due to academic motivations to understand better the human condition in all of its diversity and conditions, including that of being "gay."

2. This "letter" follows the style and format of another "letter" that I wrote for a chapter entitled "Making space in the classroom for my gay identity: A letter I've been wanting to write" in *Teaching diversity: Challenges and complexities, identities and integrity* (See Aoki 2003; forthcoming in References). As with that "letter," Ono's (1997) "A Letter/Essay I've Been Longing to Write in My Personal/Academic Voice" had a profound influence on my conceptualization and understanding of "voice." After reading and re-reading his essay, I also came to a clearer understanding of how I wanted to *use* as a scholar my voice(s) in the paths of cultural advocacy and understanding. I believe the "letter" format can be shared with family, friends, colleagues, professionals, and students and in an *accessible* and *practical* way invite conversations on the complex issue of sexual orientation/identity, interpersonal/cultural relations, and the politics of everyday life. When dealing with stigmatized cultural identities, I believe that both accessibility and practicality is its own type of advocacy for enhanced conversation and understanding. I owe a debt of gratitude to Professor Kent Ono for providing an alternative methodology for my academic writing. Finally, with the format of this essay, I have taken some liberty with APA guidelines for "aesthetic" presentation of the "letter."

3. I have changed the names of individuals in this essay for reasons of confidentiality. Although the lives, including my own, which are noted in this letter are/were "out" in many contexts, I realize that we still live in stigmatized times with regard to diversity, particularly in that of being "gay." Hence, the names used are pseudonyms with the exception of my own, Eric.

4. I use the term "relational connection" because I was not and have not been "married" or "unionized" with either of my romantic partners. A friend of mine gifted me this alternative terminology when speaking of my relational life; nonetheless, I recognize that the cultural-political "symbol use" for advancing or attending to policy re-

quires a more "traditional" negotiation of language use. Trevor and I often spoke of our connection as one of being "with." Although he and I never had a "union" ceremony (which is presently available in certain pockets of the world), we supported that right and recognition for those who desire it in their lifetimes. We also voiced support for "gay" individuals who wanted "marriage" as well. We shared a belief in fair and just treatment and recognition for Lesbian, Gay, Bisexual, Transgender (LGBT) individuals who are partnered together in life, a treatment and recognition that should not be second to any "one" model of love and commitment. Ryan believes much the same, yet he in his lifetime, desires (and deserves) a "union" or some "publicly" recognized ceremony. At this point in our lives, relationally, Ryan and I are much too "young" to know if that relational path is for us. Regardless, Ryan has been a relational partner-friend extraordinaire, and we are in love.

5. Here, I use Murray (1996) and note my distinction from the "general" descriptions given of individuals in various ethnic co-cultures. Murray (1996) is careful to note in his section entitled "Some Cautions" that we can of course find general trends and individual differences within gay, ethnic co-cultures of the United States. He also recognizes the need for caution so as to avoid speaking for others. Although I typically do not conduct cultural-etic research, I appreciate his book for advancing conversations about ethnic diversity in U.S. "American" gay lives.

REFERENCES

Aoki, E. (2003). Making space in the classroom for my gay identity: A letter I've been wanting to write. In *Teaching diversity: Challenges and complexities, identities and integrity*. Timpson, B., Canetto, S., Borrayo, E., & Yang, R. (Eds.). Madison, Wisconsin: Atwood Publishing.

Martin, J. N., & Nakayama, T. K. (2000). *Intercultural communication in contexts*. (2nd ed.). Mountain View, CA: Mayfield Publishing Company.

Murray, S. O. (1996). *American Gay*. Chicago, IL: The University of Chicago Press.

Ono, K. A. (1997, Winter). A letter/essay I've been longing to write in my personal/academic voice. *Western Journal of Communication, 6,* (1). 114-125.

Palmer, R., & Bor, R. (2001). The challenges to intimacy and sexual relationships for gay men in HIV serodiscordant relationships: A pilot study. *Journal of Marital and Family Therapy, 27,* (4). 419-431.

Signorile, M. (1997). *Life outside*. New York, NY: HarperPerrenial.

Stewart, J. & Logan, C. (1998). *Together: Communicating interpersonally*. (5th ed.). Boston, MA: McGraw Hill Companies, Inc.

Sullivan, A. (1998). *Love undetectable: Notes on friendship, sex, and survival*. New York, NY: Alfred A. Knopf.

Warner, M. (1999). *The trouble with normal: Sex, politics and the ethics of queer life*. New York, NY: The Free Press.

Wat, E. C. (2002). *The making of a gay Asian community: An oral history of Pre-AIDS Los Angeles*. Boulder, CO: Rowman & Littlefield Publishers, Inc.

The Sexual Orientation Matrix for Supervision: A Tool for Training Therapists to Work with Same-Sex Couples

Janie K. Long
Elizabeth Lindsey

SUMMARY. The Sexual Orientation Matrix for Supervision (SOMS) was created in order to assist supervisors and trainers in preparing supervisees to work with lesbian, gay, and bisexual (LGB) clients. The

Janie K. Long, PhD, Department of Applied Psychology, Antioch New England Graduate School, Keene, NH 03431-3512 (E-mail: Janie_Long@antiochne.edu). Elizabeth Lindsey, PhD, is affiliated with the School of Social Work, The University of North Carolina-Greensboro.

Address correspondence to: Janie K. Long, Department of Applied Psychology, Antioch New England Graduate School, Keene, NH 03431-3512 (E-mail: Janie_Long@antiochne.edu).

The authors wish to acknowledge the input of Damond Dotson, PhD, and Jenny Manders, PhD, in the early development of this manuscript. The authors also wish to acknowledge our indebtedness to our LGBT clients and our supervisees who have contributed significantly to the development of our own thinking and growth in this area.

[Haworth co-indexing entry note]: "The Sexual Orientation Matrix for Supervision: A Tool for Training Therapists to Work with Same-Sex Couples." Long, Janie, K., and Elizabeth Lindsey. Co-published simultaneously in *Journal of Couple & Relationship Therapy* (The Haworth Press) Vol. 3, No. 2/3, 2004, pp. 123-135; and: *Relationship Therapy with Same-Sex Couples* (ed: Jerry J. Bigner, and Joseph L. Wetchler) The Haworth Press, Inc., 2004, pp. 123-135. Single or multiple copies of this article are available for a fee from The Haworth Document Delivery Service [1-800-HAWORTH, 9:00 a.m. - 5:00 p.m. (EST). E-mail address: docdelivery@haworthpress.com].

http://www.haworthpress.com/web/JCRT
Digital Object Identifier: 10.1300/J398v03n02_12

SOMS was developed around two core concepts: (1) degree of heterosexual bias, and (2) degree of acceptance of LGB orientations and behavior. Supervisors can employ the matrix to explore both their own and their supervisee's levels of comfort, knowledge, and experience in working with LGB clients including same-sex couples. This article describes the development of the matrix, an exploration of the concepts underlying this tool, and an explanation of how to use the matrix, including suggested tasks for supervision of therapists working with same-sex couples. *[Article copies available for a fee from The Haworth Document Delivery Service: 1-800-HAWORTH. E-mail address: <docdelivery@haworthpress.com> Website: <http://www.HaworthPress.com> © 2004 by The Haworth Press, Inc. All rights reserved.]*

KEYWORDS. Sexual orientation, supervision, training

It is estimated that approximately 50 million people in the United States are lesbian, gay, or bisexual (LGB), or are closely related to someone who is (Patterson, 1995). A recent random sample of 457 clinical members of the American Association for Marriage and Family Therapy indicated that 72% of the respondents reported one-tenth of their practices included lesbian and gay clients (Green & Bobele, 1994). Yet, many authors have questioned the preparedness of family therapists to deal with LGBT clients (Laird & Green, 1995; Long, 1996; Long & Serovich, 2003; Ritter & Terndrup, 2002). Doherty and Simmons (1996) found that a little more than 50% of marriage and family therapists (MFTs; $N = 526$) felt competent in treating lesbians and gay men. Malley and Tasker (1999) suggest, ". . . family therapy in general has been slow to consider sexuality as an influence on family life, and in particular to address the issues raised by families led by a lesbian or gay parent or a lesbian or gay couple" (p. 3).

It has been the experience of both authors that trainees from across the mental health disciplines are inadequately prepared to deal with LGB clients and their families. Even those students who feel that they are well prepared are often limited in knowledge, skills, and/or experience. Are mental health training faculties reluctant to deal with this topic or just ill prepared to do so? We suggest that both these reasons are plausible given that issues of same-sex relationships and sexual identity were probably rarely addressed when many current faculty were in training. Thus, their comfort level and knowledge base are likely to be limited (Long & Serovich, 2003).

Supervisors and trainers who are committed to preparing supervisees to work with a diverse client population will want to ensure that supervisees have both an adequate knowledge base and clinical skills to work with lesbian, gay, and bisexual clients. Brown (1991) suggests that when supervisors fail to introduce supervisees to LGB issues, do not encourage supervisee self-examination regarding sexual orientation, and fail to do consciousness raising regarding sexual minorities,[1] they allow ". . . the development of professionals who are not only deficient in their ability to work with sexual minorities . . . but in the creation of therapists who are uncomfortable with ambiguities and questions regarding sexuality" (p. 237). Supervisors who address issues related to sexual orientation encourage supervisees to learn about and accept differences and develop an awareness of their personal biases regarding sexual orientation.

DEVELOPMENT OF THE SEXUAL ORIENTATION MATRIX FOR SUPERVISION

The Sexual Orientation Matrix for Supervision (SOMS) evolved out of discussions between a supervisor and three supervisors-in-training, while we were conducting supervision of therapy with LGBT clients. We were struggling with how to discuss with our supervisees a topic about which most persons socialized in the United States have intense feelings (Greene, 1994). We realized that just as supervisees approach lesbian, bisexual, and gay clients with varying levels of acceptance, comfort, and knowledge, so did we as supervisors. We wanted to examine our own biases in order to work more honestly and effectively with our supervisees, as well as with any future LGB clients. We agreed that not talking with supervisees about this topic would be unethical, both from a training standpoint and in the interest of the welfare of the clients. Establishing and maintaining trust and mutual respect and providing a safe environment for the supervisees to examine their beliefs was foremost in our minds (Long, 1997). We were interested in exploring with supervisees their levels of comfort in working with sexual minority clients, as well as their levels of experience and knowledge of the gay community including same-sex couple relationships, gay and lesbian parenting, and historical, social, and legal trends.

In recent years, the literature related to working with LGB clients in therapy has increased (Bepko & Johnson, 2000; Bernstein, 2000; Greene, 1994; Kurdek, 1994; Ritter & Terndrup, 2002). We found little specific guidance, however, about how to deal with these issues in supervision especially when there were potential differences in values and beliefs between supervisors and trainees. We began meeting as a group to discuss how we could best supervise trainees working with this client population. Our discussions often revolved around two core concepts: (1) the degree of heterosexual bias, and (2) the degree of acceptance of lesbian, gay, and bisexual orientations and behaviors.

Heterosexual Bias

Heterosexual bias, a form of multicultural bias, has the potential to harm future clients and supervisees (Long, 1996). Heterosexual bias has been defined as, ". . . conceptualizing human experience in strictly heterosexual terms and consequently ignoring, invalidating, or derogating lesbian, gay, and bisexual orientations, behaviors, relationships, and lifestyles" (Herek, Kimmel, Amaro, & Melton, 1991, p. 958). Heterosexism is an ethnocentric lens through which much of the culture has traditionally viewed the world (Long, 1997). This heterosexist lens has historically been employed by mental health professionals to evaluate, analyze, research, and work in therapy with lesbians, gays, and bisexuals. Evidence of the presence of heterosexism in the mental health arena includes the following beliefs: (a) heterosexuality is normal and healthy and gay, lesbian, and bisexual orientations are deviant or pathological (Brown, 1989); (b) the assumption that theories and research findings based on studies of heterosexuals are applicable and generalizable to gays, bisexuals, and lesbians (Kitzinger, 1987); and (c) the presumption that heterosexuality and its accompanying lifestyle provide normative standards against which the lives of lesbians, gays, and bisexuals need to be compared in order to be understood (Cabaj, 1988; Goodrich, Rampage, Ellman, & Halstead, 1988).

Levels of Acceptance

Both supervisors and supervisees possess varying levels of acceptance of lesbian, gay, and bisexual orientations. These levels of acceptance can be manifested both consciously and unconsciously during the supervisory process. Some supervisors and supervisees view gays, lesbians, and bisexuals negatively, perhaps even as repulsive, immoral, or sick, and encourage supervisees to establish the goal of therapy as changing the person's orientation (Rosik, 2003). Other supervisors or supervisees consider bisexuals, gays, and lesbians to be developmentally stymied from reaching their "full heterosexual" potential (Yarhouse, 1998). These supervisors would focus on ways therapists can encourage their clients to "grow out of it." The potential for "becoming straight" is thus reinforced in supervision. Some supervisees display a pseudo-accepting attitude of "I can work with gays, lesbians, and bisexuals in therapy as long as it is not the focus of our work." Therapy would be characterized by statements like: "You're not a lesbian to me, you are a person," and "I'm very comfortable in interacting with you so let's not focus on your sexual orientation." These supervisees dismiss sexual orientation as an issue to be addressed (Long, 1997).

Other supervisees and supervisors may be accepting of lesbian, bisexual, and gay orientations but, due to a lack of knowledge and/or exposure, are unaware of having heterosexual bias. Once heterosexism is discovered, they are willing to examine their own attitudes, values, and behaviors. Some supervisors and supervisees value diversity in relationships and see sexual minorities as a valid part of that diversity and as indispensable in our society. They are willing to become allies and advocates to ensure that gays, lesbians, and bisexuals prosper in society. These supervisors encourage therapists to work with sexual minority clients and to increase their knowledge and skills with this group.

THE SEXUAL ORIENTATION MATRIX FOR SUPERVISION

Because we believed that levels of acceptance and heterosexual bias were intertwined, we developed a matrix to help us examine how these two concepts might, in combination, influence the supervision process (see Figure 1). The vertical axis represents the level of heterosexual bias, and the horizontal axis indicates the person's level of acceptance of LGB orientations, lifestyles, and behaviors. In this way, we attempted to account for both beliefs/values (heterosexual bias) and behavior (level of acceptance). The quadrants represent four intersections of levels of bias and acceptance. We do not believe that persons always fall neatly into one of these quadrants but rather that beliefs and values are more discontinuous and pastiched than steady state. However, we developed the matrix as a beginning tool for supervisors and supervisees to explore these issues.

The quadrants[2] are as follows:

Quadrant A

Persons are very nonaccepting of LGB sexual orientations and/or behaviors and are very heterosexist in their behavior. These persons are likely to vilify lesbian, gay, and bisexual orientations, relationships, and lifestyles. Issues that therapists and supervisees in this quadrant might face when working with gay and lesbian couples include:

Therapist Issues

- Do I want to work with gay and lesbian couples?
- If not, do I feel the freedom to say so? What are the ramifications of being honest about my feelings with my supervisor?
- Do I want to learn more about gay and lesbian relationships?

Supervisor Issues

- Is it ethical to allow the therapist who falls in this quadrant to work with same-sex couples?
- If this therapist wants to work gay and lesbian couples, is s/he trying to undermine their relationship or change someone's sexual orientation, consciously or unconsciously?

FIGURE 1. The Sexual Orientation Matrix for Supervision

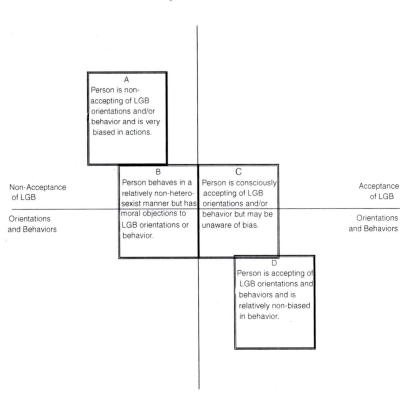

- Is it acceptable for the therapist to decline to learn about lesbian and gay couples?

Quadrant B

Persons behave in a relatively nonheterosexist manner, but have moral objections to LGB sexual orientations and/or behaviors.

Therapist Issues

- Do I want to work with same-sex couples? Can I be effective considering my moral objections to their sexual orientation?

- If I do want to work with them, what are my motivations? Am I interested in undermining relationships or changing sexual orientation?
- Can I work with gay and lesbian couples around issues that are not related to their sexual orientation? What would I do if subsequently sexual orientation became an important factor in the work we were doing?
- If I decide I will not work with same-sex couples, how do I handle the situation when I learn that a potential client or a client I have been seeing is gay, lesbian, or bisexual? What if I decided I needed to do couple therapy with them after I had already begun therapy?
- Should I tell my same-sex couples my feelings about their sexual orientation? Is it ethical to work with them if I do not?

Supervisor Issues

- How do I talk with a therapist about how his/her moral objections might influence the therapeutic relationship and direction?
- Can therapists who morally disapprove of gay, lesbian, and bisexual sexual orientations effectively work with these couples on any issue?
- Is it ethical to allow a therapist to work with same-sex couples if they morally disapprove of their sexual orientation, even if the person is respectful in their attitude and demeanor toward the clients?
- How do I determine when or if to encourage therapists to work with lesbian and gay couples with whom they may feel uncomfortable? How do I discover the nature of their uncomfortableness?
- How do I prepare therapists to refer same-sex couples?

Quadrant C

Persons are consciously accepting of LGB sexual orientations and/or behaviors, but are unaware of heterosexist bias that manifests in their behavior.

Therapist Issues

- What blind spots do I have in terms of my biases, and how are they manifested in my thinking about and working with gay and lesbian couples?
- What knowledge and skills do I need to be more effective with same-sex couples?
- What can I do to gain more exposure to lesbian and gay couples?
- How well does my model(s) of therapy allow me to address issues, which may be encountered in same-sex relationships, e.g., oppression, invisibility, discrimination, and hate crimes?

Supervisor Issues

- How and when do I provide needed information for students about same-sex relationships?

- How have I fostered relationships with the gay, lesbian, and bisexual community so trainees will have the opportunity to work with same-sex couples?
- How effective am I at recognizing unconscious heterosexual biases on the part of therapists and helping them to address these issues?

Quadrant D

Persons are very accepting of LGB sexual orientations and/or behaviors and are relatively nonheterosexist in behavior.

Therapist Issues

- What knowledge and skills do I need to be more effective with same-sex couples?
- What can I do to gain more exposure to lesbian and gay couples?
- How well does my model(s) of therapy allow me to address issues, which may be encountered in same-sex relationships, e.g., oppression, invisibility, discrimination, and hate crimes?
- Do I have unconscious biases that affect my working with gay, lesbian, and bisexual clients (this is a lower priority than for therapists in Quadrant C)?

Supervisor Issues

- Does my knowledge of the therapist's openness toward gays, lesbians, and bisexuals cause me to assume that the therapist is totally unbiased when working with same-sex couples?
- What can I learn from this supervisee who may know more about same-sex couples and the issues they face than I do?

UTILIZING THE MATRIX

Supervisor Self-Assessment

Family therapy supervisors are not immune to the influence of the ubiquitous existence of heterosexist bias in the dominant culture (Long & Serovich, 2003). Heterosexism can be exhibited in many ways including: outright prejudice or discrimination; ignorance of the special issues of gays, bisexuals, and lesbians; stereotypical thought processes; and insensitivity. Therefore, self-examination is an important step in preparing to work with supervisees around issues of heterosexism and sexual orientation. This matrix has been designed to provide supervisors with a tool that can be used to prompt self-examination as well as to work with supervisees.

Self-examination of heterosexism on the part of the supervisor may occur as the result of self-awareness of bias or may occur as a result of interactions within the supervisory process. This awareness might be prompted in several ways including: (a) a supervisee who differs from the supervisor in acceptance of gays, lesbians, and bisexuals; (b) a supervisor who discovers that she or he has inadequate knowledge related to *HIV/AIDS* in the advisement of a supervisee concerning a case; or (c) a supervisee who encourages a bisexual client to adopt a straight lifestyle and ignores the fact that the person has identified as bisexual (Long, 1996). Supervisors can then employ the matrix to begin to scrutinize their own levels of bias and acceptance by placing themselves in a quadrant of the matrix and identifying the issues they need to address related to their location on the matrix. Some possible questions for supervisors to ask themselves related to their own knowledge, skills, beliefs, and practices include:

Knowledge

- Have I consistently read publications on working with LGB clients and couples in therapy? Is my knowledge base current?
- Am I aware of the suggested best practices in working with LGB clients including the guidelines provided by my professional organizations, e.g., most major mental health organizations (ACA, APA, NASW) have taken a strong stance against the practice of reparative therapy.
- How much have I read about LGB lifestyles and relationships including their historical struggles with oppression and discrimination? Have I considered the multiple levels of discrimination experienced by inter-racial and intercultural lesbian and gay couples?
- How many personal and professional relationships have I had with lesbians, gays, and bisexuals?

Skill

- How comfortable am I in working with same-sex couples?
- How much experience do I have with these couples and families?
- How comfortable am I and how much experience do I have in working with LGB supervisees?

Stereotypical Thought Processes

- Do I equate same-sex attraction with pathology (use terms like sexual deviants)?
- Have I examined my own use of language for heterosexual bias. For example, when comparing gay or lesbian couples and families to other family types, do I use parallel terms such as "heterosexual couples" as opposed to "normal couples"?
- Do I assume that clients and supervisees are heterosexual?

Discriminatory Practices

- Do I encourage the acceptance and employment of sexual minorities in the work environment?
- Do I use examples in supervision that include same-sex couples being careful not to only present them as dysfunctional?
- Do I include partners in social functions; recognize commitment ceremonies between partners; display understanding during the illness or death of a partner or co-parented children; support insurance coverage and other benefits for partners and any co-parented children?
- Do I ask LGB supervisees to cover holidays because "they don't have to worry about family" (Long, 1997)?

Using the Matrix for Supervision

Once supervisors have examined their own values, beliefs, knowledge, and skills, they can move into helping supervisees examine their issues in working with same-sex couples. The matrix can be discussed with the supervisee as a standard part of supervision or employed when the supervisee first begins to work with sexual minority clients. Initially, the supervisor and supervisee could spend time discussing the supervisee's level of comfort in working with clients from varied backgrounds. As no other time in the history of the U.S., there is an increased chance that supervisees will work with couples from varied racial and cultural backgrounds. Pearlman (1996) suggests that lesbians, like everyone else, are meeting and entering into relationships with women from varied cultural backgrounds including race, ethnicity, and class. The same could be speculated about gay male couples.

As a part of the above discussion the matrix could be used to focus on sexual orientation. We believe that it is helpful for supervisees to know where their supervisors place themselves on the matrix and how they believe it affects their ability to supervise these cases. Supervisors can encourage supervisees to pinpoint the sources of their discomfort (lack of knowledge, lack of exposure, conflict with personal values, lack of skill, ties to their own personal experience). It should be noted, however, that even though a personal examination of one's own beliefs and biases is necessary, supervisees might not choose to share all reflections with their supervisors.[3]

When supervisors and supervisees have very different levels of acceptance and bias, supervisors should explore how those differences will affect their supervision on any given case. For example, a supervisor who places themselves in quadrants A or B may not be effective when supervising a LGB supervisee, particularly with same-sex couples. Likewise, a LGB supervisor may feel uncomfortable supervising persons who place themselves in quadrants A or B. In addition to bringing forth both therapist's and supervisor's issues, the matrix also offers a beginning point for developing tasks of supervision when working with LGB clients. Some of the potential learning tasks for supervisees in each quadrant include:

Quadrant A

- Substantive knowledge building (aspects of gay, lesbian, and bisexual orientations, lifestyles, and relationships).
- Identification and clarification of biases and their origins.
- Opportunities for the therapist to observe other clinicians working with gays, lesbians, and bisexuals (e.g., behind the mirror or videos).

Quadrant B

- Help therapist identify under what circumstances a referral should be made and under what circumstances, if any, s/he can work with same-sex couples.
- Focus on how therapists can communicate their decision to not work with same-sex couples.
- If the therapist and supervisor agree that the therapist will work with lesbian and gay couples, supervision should focus on how to minimize the likelihood that heterosexual bias will be manifested in the therapy and on knowledge building concerning gay, lesbian, and bisexual issues, as well as specific treatment issues.

Quadrant C

- Identification and clarification of therapist's unconscious heterosexist biases (high priority).
- Substantive knowledge building concerning special issues in gay, lesbian, and bisexual relationships and identity development.
- Knowledge building concerning treatment issues and strategies.

Quadrant D

- Substantive knowledge building concerning special issues in gay, lesbian, and bisexual relationships and identity development.
- Knowledge building concerning treatment issues and strategies.
- Continuing identification of conscious and unconscious areas of heterosexism (lower priority than in Quadrant C).
- Encourage therapists to reflect on the process by which they have been able to minimize heterosexual bias.

CONCLUSION

As noted previously, we developed the Sexual Orientation Matrix for Supervision to assist supervisors in preparing supervisees to work with lesbian, gay, and bisexual clients, including same-sex couples. We caution the reader to remember that sexualities are fluid and pastiched, therefore, the matrix is best utilized not as a fixed instrument but as a starting point for exploration (Simon, 1996). We have found it to be a very valuable tool in facilitating discussions around the issues of sexual orientation, both among ourselves as supervisors and with our supervisees. On occasion, we have also employed the matrix with our bisexual, lesbian, and gay clients who, just as heterosexuals, have been influenced by a heterosexist society. In these instances the matrix was implemented to examine clients' levels of self-acceptance and bias, thus providing important insight into the stories they told themselves about who they were. Through our employment of the matrix, we have encouraged supervisees and ourselves to honestly examine who we are and what we believe, to learn about and accept differences, to develop an awareness of personal biases regarding sexual orientation, and to learn ways to work more effectively and respectfully with same-sex couples.

NOTES

1. The term, sexual minority, is used with caution in recognition of the belief that sexual orientation for humans is fluid and changeable. Therefore, it is difficult to determine who is in the minority. For further discussion of this topic see Simon (1996).

2. The quadrants are designated by the letters A,B,C, and D in order to avoid the use of labels.

3. For further discussion of the potential complications of self-disclosure see Laird and Green, 1995 and Long, 1996.

REFERENCES

Bepko, C., & Johnson, T. (2000). Gay and lesbian couples in therapy: Perspectives for the contemporary family therapist. *Journal of Marital and Family Therapy, 26,* 409-419.

Berstein, A. C. (2000). Straight therapists working with lesbians and gays in family therapy. *Journal of Marital and Family Therapy, 26,* 443-454.

Brown, L. S. (1991) Commentary on the special issue of *The Counseling Psychologist: Counseling with lesbians and gay men. The Counseling Psychologist, 19,* 235-238.

Brown, L. S. (1989). New voices, new visions: Toward a lesbian/gay paradigm for psychology. *Psychology of Women Quarterly, 13,* 445-456.

Brown, L. S., & Zimmer, D. (1986). An introduction to therapy issues of lesbian and gay male couples. In N. S. Jacobson & A. S. Gurman (Eds.), *Clinical handbook of marital therapy.* (pp. 451-468). New York: The Guilford Press.

Cabaj, R. P. (1988). Homosexuality and neurosis: Considerations for psychotherapy. *Journal of Homosexuality, 15,* 13-23.

Goodrich, T. J., Rampage, C., Ellman, B., & Halstead, K. (1988). *Feminist family therapy: A casebook.* New York: W. W. Norton & Co.

Green, R. J. (1996). Learning about lesbians and gays. *Family Process, 35.*

Green, S. K., & Bobele, M. (1994). Family therapists' response to AIDS: An examination of attitudes, knowledge, and contact. *Journal of Marital and Family Therapy, 20,* 349-367.

Greene, B. (1994). Lesbian and gay sexual orientations: Implications for clinical training, practice, and research. In B. Greene & G. M. Herek (Eds.), *Lesbian and gay psychology: Theory, research, and clinical implications* (pp. 1-24). Thousand Oaks, CA: Sage.

Herek, G. M., Kimmel, D. C., Amaro, H., & Melton, G. B. (1991). Avoiding heterosexist bias in psychological research. *American Psychologist, 46,* 957-963.

Kitzinger, C. (1987). *The social construction of lesbianism.* London: Sage.

Kurdek, L. A. (1994). *Social services for gay and lesbian couples.* New York: The Haworth Press, Inc.

Laird, J., & Green, R. J. (1995). Introduction. *Journal of Feminist Family Therapy, 7,* 3-13.

Long, J. K. (1996). Working with lesbians, gays, and bisexuals: Addressing heterosexism in supervision. *Family Process, 35,* 1-6.

Long, J. K. (1997). Lesbian, gay, and bisexual orientations: Implications for the supervisory process (pp. 59-71). In C. Storm & T. Todd (Eds.), *The complete systemic supervisor: Philosophy, methods and contexts,* New York: Allyn & Bacon.

Long, J. K., & Serovich, J. M. (2003). Incorporating sexual orientation into MFT training programs: Infusion and inclusion. *Journal of Marital and Family Therapy, 29,* 59-68.

Malley, M., & Tasker, F. (1999). Lesbians, gay men and family therapy: A contradiction in terms? *Journal of Family Therapy, 21,* 3-29.

Patterson, C. (1995). Sexual orientation and human development: An overview. *Developmental Psychology, 31,* 3-11.

Pearlman, S. F. (1996). Loving across race and class divides: Relational challenges and the interracial lesbian couple. In M. Hill & E.D. Rothblum (Eds.), *Couples therapy: Feminist perspectives* (pp. 25-35). New York, NY: The Haworth Press, Inc.

Ritter, K.Y., & Terndrup, A. I. (2002). *Handbook of affirmative psychotherapy with lesbians and gay men.* New York: The Guilford Press.

Rosik, C. H. (2003). Motivational, ethical, and epistemological foundations in the treatment of unwanted homoerotic attraction. *Journal of Marital and Family Therapy, 29,* 13-28.

Roth, S. (1989). Psychotherapy with lesbian couples: Individual issues, female socialization, and the social context. In M. McGoldrick, C. M. Anderson, & F. Walsh (Eds.), *Women in families: A framework for family therapy* (pp. 286-307). New York: Norton.

Simon, W. (1996). *Postmodern sexualities.* New York: Routledge.

Yarhouse, M. A. (1998). When clients seek treatment for same-sex attraction: Ethical issues in the "right to choose" debate. *Psychotherapy, 35,* 248-259.

A Heterosexual Therapist's Journey Toward Working with Same-Sex Couples

Joseph L. Wetchler

SUMMARY. This paper presents the thoughts and ethical problems faced by a heterosexual therapist who works with same sex couples. It discusses the mistakes made throughout his career as a clinician, and provides advice for others based on these experiences. *[Article copies available for a fee from The Haworth Document Delivery Service: 1-800-HAWORTH. E-mail address: <docdelivery@haworthpress.com> Website: <http://www. HaworthPress.com> © 2004 by The Haworth Press, Inc. All rights reserved.]*

KEYWORDS. Same-sex couples, sexual orientation, self-of-the-therapist, couple therapy, same-sex couple therapy, professional issues in therapy

I am a heterosexual therapist who works with gay, lesbian, and bisexual (GLB) clients, and same-sex couples. While this statement may seem like a presumptuous and self-serving way to start a paper, it is important in defining the therapeutic relationship when I work with GLB clients. Further, it represents many hurdles I have had to overcome to do this work.

I am aware that in writing this article, I am leaving myself open to many questions, and even angry comments from readers who do not know me, or my

---

Joseph L. Wetchler, PhD, is Professor and Program Director, Marriage and Family Therapy Program, Purdue University Calumet, Hammond, IN 46323.

[Haworth co-indexing entry note]: "A Heterosexual Therapist's Journey Toward Working with Same-Sex Couples." Wetchler, Joseph L. Co-published simultaneously in *Journal of Couple & Relationship Therapy* (The Haworth Press) Vol. 3, No. 2/3, 2004, pp. 137-145; and: *Relationship Therapy with Same-Sex Couples* (ed: Jerry J. Bigner, and Joseph L. Wetchler) The Haworth Press, Inc., 2004, pp. 137-145. Single or multiple copies of this article are available for a fee from The Haworth Document Delivery Service [1-800-HAWORTH. 9:00 a.m. - 5:00 p.m. (EST). E-mail address: docdelivery@haworthpress.com].

values. An interesting thing happens when you work with the GLB community and engage in GLB scholarship, people invariably begin to question your sexual orientation. It probably comes as no surprise to my readers that no one ever questioned if I was a closet African American when I edited a book on interracial couples (Thomas, Karis, & Wetchler, in press), yet I have raised several eyebrows and received a few snide comments about my work on this project from friends and colleagues. If you engage in GLB scholarship, or work with members of the GLB community, you must be gay! How did the presumptions and prejudices around this work become so rigid?

Some may read my statement of heterosexuality as a way to distance myself from the subject, my attempt to protect myself from a homophobic society, or possibly my fear of someone making a pass at me. While I have some fears in writing this piece, and, yes, the baring of my own homophobia is one of them, I am not that worried about being mistaken for being gay. And, how nice if someone finds me cute (However, I have never been comfortable with passes by either males or females)! My reason for writing this paper is to discuss the issues one heterosexual therapist faces in doing this work, and to make other heterosexual therapists aware of the road they might travel. One thing I can definitively say: if you are a straight therapist who plans to work with GLB clients, you will have to face your issues.

In writing this paper, I will present several clinical situations I found personally challenging. I will also discuss several of my mistakes. I will then attempt to explain what I learned from these situations, or discuss the doubts I still face. Finally, I will present some of my guidelines for working with GLB clients.

MY FIRST CASE

I am not proud to say that I totally botched my first case where same sex issues came up. But I did! It was one of my first cases after completing my master's degree twenty-four years ago, and many years before I earned my doctorate. I had been working with a single-mother around problems with her teenage daughter. After these problems were resolved, the mother chose to continue working with me on several of her personal issues. The therapy flowed easily and she had made several positive strides, when she told me she wondered whether she might be a lesbian. As she shared her thoughts, I found myself growing progressively deaf. She began to speak in a more tentative and halting manner as my hearing problem increased. Shortly after this, she changed the subject and my hearing returned.

I was horrified and ashamed of my behavior. In an attempt to rectify the situation, I sought consultation from a colleague, a homosexual therapist. Unfortunately, I found his advice to be less than helpful. Rather than tell me how to facilitate the situation, he rather sternly told me I better "strongly warn her about the pitfalls of her actions. She had to know what problems she was in for if she chose to behave in this manner." Needless to say, I left this consultation more confused than when I started. Not knowing what to do, I chose the safe path of letting her bring it up the next time. Of course, she didn't, and we continued to have a positive therapy that both of us agreed was beneficial at termination. Except, that we never got around to discussing her sexual orientation!

In completing my master's degree, I had never taken a course in human sexuality or done any specialized readings in GLB issues. Of course, at that time there was not much information available, and much of it was somewhat questionable. While I did not know it at the time, my reactions to my client came from my own homophobia, and a sense of heterosexual guilt (a sense of personal guilt that stems from being part of a heterosexual culture that demeans and persecutes members of the gay, lesbian, bisexual, and transgender community). I eventually realized, that no matter how liberal I may have felt (after all, some of my best friends were gay!?!?!), there were many issues that had been ingrained in me having been raised in a heterosexist society (one in which the dominant view of normality is based on a heterosexual paradigm). Further, no matter how hard it was to admit, I had also made my fair share of "gay jokes" growing up. To rectify this situation, I made sure to take extra coursework in human sexuality and do readings on GLB issues. Further, I also made sure to focus on my personal issues when working with GLB clients.

Another issue that contributed to this mess, was my colleague's homophobia. I never thought that he might also have problems with being gay. Boy, was I naïve! If anything, this realization might have been the most valuable silver lining in a very gray cloud. Besides my own issues, I had to come to grips with the idea that homosexuals also suffer from homophobia.

Discrimination toward homosexuals is still sanctioned in this country, no matter how many affirmative action statements may exist. Until June 2003, there were some states in which same-sex physical intimacies were illegal. Further, no state allows legal homosexual marriage, and many corporations do not provide benefits for non-married life partners. Finally, numerous religions consider it a sin to love someone who is not a member of the opposite sex. Based on all of this, the question is not how can homosexuals be homophobic, but, "How can homosexuals not be homophobic when raised in such an oppressive world?" Straight therapists need especially be aware when GLB clients ask for re-orientation therapy because they do not like being gay (Green, 2003). Re-orientation therapy is one of the components of institutional oppression. Make someone hate himself or herself enough and then offer them the cure of conversion, which of course is never a cure. The goal is not to convert, but to teach personal acceptance and self-love in spite of an oppressive society. And, of course, the larger goal is to change the society.

HETEROSEXUAL BLIND SPOTS

Because I have grown up heterosexual in a heterosexist society, I have to be aware of my personal assumptions when dealing with GLB clients (Bernstein, 2000). For example, I have always known I was heterosexual. My earliest recollection of my sexuality was of being male, and eventually of being interested in females. In fact, I barely gave these issues any thought, because they fit so seamlessly into my larger societal fabric. I could talk about my gender and sexual concerns without any fear of reprisal. I never had to worry about being accepted because I was already so accepted that I never gave it a thought. Stone Fish and Coole (2002) created a list of questions about coming to awareness of one's own gender and sexuality, and are an excellent resource for heterosexuals to realize the difference between how they and homosexuals develop their sexual and gendered sense of self. In fact, it is crucial to understand how GLB sexuality develops in a rather confusing manner in a hostile environment.

Over the years, I have realized how much my clients might lose by sharing their homosexuality with others, and more importantly, the fear they have of sharing themselves with me. To facilitate this process, I must be open about my sexuality and my personal values to my GLB clients. Further, I share that I have blind spots because of being so seamlessly integrated into heterosexist culture. I make it clear that at times I may mess up, and at times I may need to be taught about some things that I don't understand. I often put aside my expert role and work collaboratively with my clients (Anderson, 1997; White 1995).

While I try to deal with my biases, I still make mistakes I might not make if I was more aware. I once developed an erotic fantasy in a couple I was seeing for marriage therapy to put some spark into their dead sex life, only to find that the husband became aroused toward me. After his slip, we both stared at each other unable to speak. I, because I was totally caught off guard, and I presume he, because he realized he had come close to outing himself when his wife did not know, and that he realized that I did know. At the end of the session, he stated his dissatisfaction with the therapy saying it did not deal with the real issues. The couple terminated therapy, and was never heard from again.

How could I have missed this! I had seen the couple for several sessions and never once thought that he might be gay or bisexual. I realized that I automatically assumed that all opposite-sex couples that came to me were actually heterosexual. In fact, I never questioned it. But of course, this is not the case. How many closeted GLB's had come to my practice claiming to have a marital problem, when in fact there were core issues with sexual orientation.

I now am more aware when working with couples. In fact, I ask questions about same-sex orientation as part of my assessment. I typically do this during individual sessions with partners when I also ask about issues like abuse and affairs.

GRAY AREAS

I often find that working with the GLB community leads me to gray-area issues that are not in the textbooks. Sometimes I am left to wing it and hope that my instincts are correct. The following case is one such example. And, while it had a fairly positive outcome, it haunts me to this day.

A woman called requesting marital therapy for her husband and her, but asked for an individual session before they came as a couple. During the appointment, she told me that she was a lesbian, but discovered it after her marriage. She stated that she was comfortable with her lesbianism and had no desire to change her orientation. She reported that she had several relationships with women over several stormy years in her marriage and that her husband was aware of them. In fact they had dealt with her lesbianism and her affairs in a previous therapy. She also stated that the majority of the last therapy focused on her lesbianism. This time, she wanted to focus on their marriage, and nothing else. Even though she was a lesbian, she loved her husband and wanted to make her marriage work. Further, she had been totally monogamous since their last therapy, which took place 15 years ago. Regarding her sex life, she was clear that while she enjoyed sex with women more than men, she loved the intimacy she shared with her husband when they made love. She and her husband had been married 25 years, and their only daughter was married with a child of her own.

I found myself highly conflicted by this request, and shared this with her. I told her I was concerned that she wanted re-orientation therapy, which I would not do, and offered instead to help her accept her lesbianism. I also shared that I was not sure she could be truly happy in a heterosexual marriage. She told me that she was comfortable with who she was, and did not want to change her sexual orientation. What she wanted was to make her marriage work. She loved her husband, and wanted to give it her best shot. She was also clear, that if the marriage could not be saved, she would seek partnership with other women.

This was not a situation I had encountered before. It was clear that she was independently financially stable, so was not trying to hold the relationship together due to a financial power imbalance, and it was clear that she loved her husband. Since she was adamant about what she wanted, and did not want to change her sexual orientation, I agreed to see her and her husband for marital therapy.

The therapy went quite smoothly and the couple resolved most of their problems; however, they were always resistant to discuss sexual orientation, whenever I brought it up. I continued to discuss whether this was what the woman really wanted, and she always was adamant on making the marriage work. Still, I continued to be conflicted about this case and sought consultation with several sources. Needless to say, I never found consensus. Some therapists felt that while I was not doing re-orientation therapy, I was helping this woman live a lie, and keeping her from coming to grips with her true identity. Others felt I was cheating the husband, as he would continue living with a woman who could never truly find him to be a primary love object, and might someday leave him for a woman. Still others felt I had helped the woman forge a bisexual identity, which could make both her husband and her happy in a monogamous relationship. And then others felt it was a gray area in life and if the relationship made sense to the couple, it was okay to proceed.

I still question myself several years after this case. Should I have stuck with my values and refused to see the couple? Would I have approached the case differently if I were gay? Did my heterosexist view of the world blind me to other options? Further, by presenting this case, do I promote the fiction that gays and lesbians can make heterosexual unions work if they just try hard enough? I can't answer any of these questions. Yet, I continue to think about this case, and wonder if I should have proceeded differently.

I suspect that several readers will have rather strong opinions about the case, and possibly about me as a therapist. In fact, I hope this case brings about several discussions. For it is only through continued discussion and constant sharing that answers become available and gray areas move into the light.

HOW I DEVELOP COMMON GROUND WITH SAME SEX COUPLES

After presenting several of my problem cases, some readers might question how a heterosexual (or, at least I) could ever work with same sex couples. Certainly my heterosexual orientation has been a stumbling block, but it also offers me an outsider's perspective, which can be invaluable. I present here some guidelines I use, many of which were learned through the "school of hard knocks."

Sharing My Values

When a same-sex couple approaches me for therapy, I always discuss my heterosexual orientation during the first session. I discuss my openness to working with them, but also share how my heterosexist blind spots might keep me from understanding certain aspects of their lives. I ask that they be open to teaching me if we should stumble across a blind spot or if I simply do not understand something. I am comfortable not always being the expert and find that sharing my growth areas lead to a more trusting relationship. Further, the couple now has the option to continue with me, or to find someone else if they are not comfortable with my orientation.

Relating as an Outsider

I am not gay or bisexual, and I will never have the experience of dealing with the world as a same-sex oriented man. I will never understand what it is like to feel so much oppression simply for loving someone of the same sex. And, I will never experience internalized homophobia because I am gay. This gulf will always exist between my GLB clients and me, and I am clear about this with them.

What I do to bridge this gap is identify how I have felt when I have been an oppressed outsider. In this case, I relate to my feelings in being a Jew. Now, in no way am I saying there is a direct relationship between Judaism and homosexuality. My Rabbi would certainly be interested in my theological rationale (as would many non-Jewish GLB's), if I was. But I can find common ground in that both groups share oppression as outsiders. I can then empathize with my feelings and show I understand what it is like to be persecuted, and at times to wish I was not who I am.

I often help heterosexual supervisees relate to their GLB clients by having them remember those times in their lives when they were outsiders. Even if it is to remember when they were teased as children, or when they were refused entrance to a club. One trainee remembered how it felt to be an American woman in a country that hated Americans. This is not to say that many of these experiences are equal to the persecution faced by GLB's, but it helps trainees understand what it is like to be oppressed and to empathize with the feelings of their clients.

How I Deal with My Homophobia and Heterosexual Guilt

At this point in time, it is impossible for a straight therapist to be completely free of homophobia. It is so ingrained in our culture, and our sexual identities have developed so seamlessly, that we will suffer from blind spots (Bernstein, 2000; Long, 1996). This can also lead to heterosexual guilt when faced with these realizations. Homophobic responses and heterosexual guilt can paralyze therapists when working with the GLB community, as happened to me in my first case example. Besides gaining more information through reading and training, and working on my personal issues, I have found the relational ethics of contextual therapy (Boszormenyi-Nagy & Krasner, 1986) to be especially helpful in dealing with my own homophobia and heterosexual guilt.

Contextual therapists believe that we become destructively entitled (a loss of self-esteem, openness, and flexibility in dealing with others) when we receive problematic messages about ourselves from our families of origin and the society in which we are raised. The more we are destructively entitled (by receiving these messages, and taking them on as part of our personhood) the more we are limited in our ability to engage in meaningful dialogue with others. We become more destructively entitled if we then impose these problematic messages on others, or engage in limited actions with others based on these messages. While we have the right to bear a grudge for the messages we receive, we do not have the ethical right to pass them on to others or limit our interactions with others based on these messages. In fact, we only limit ourselves more. Thus, we destructively entitle our GLB clients by giving them more negative messages about themselves if we are unable to emotionally connect with them. Further, if heterosexual therapists are paralyzed by heterosexual guilt when dealing with GLB clients, they only paralyze themselves more by the guilt of having failed to emotionally connect, and how they might have hurt their clients in the process.

We can only gain constructive entitlement (positive self-esteem, openness, and flexibility in dealing with others) when we recognize how we continue to pass these messages on and attempt to do something about it. We can do this in two interrelated ways. First, we attempt to change our behaviors with those that we have destructively entitled by discontinuing those messages or behaviors with them and engaging in open and meaningful dialogue. In this case, we need to talk openly about our homophobia and heterosexim with our GLB clients, and develop plans to deal with these issues should they arise in therapy. It puts the therapeutic relationship on a more honest and open level in which both therapist and client can learn from the interaction.

Second, we begin to resolve our destructive entitlement with our families of origin and the society, which passed these messages on to us. In relationship to homophobia and heterosexual guilt, heterosexual therapists can first deal with this issue by recognizing their homophobia and opening themselves up to relational dialogue with the GLB community and their GLB clients. This can be done partially through training, but is dependant on relational dialogue. We can only learn through intimate discussion with others, in this case members of the GLB community, and through our willingness to learn from our GLB clients. The more we open ourselves up to discussion with members of the GLB community, the more we learn about ourselves, and our homophobic issues. As we face our issues, we become less constricted by heterosexual guilt and more open to dealing flexibly and intimately with our GLB clients.

Further, it is important that heterosexual therapists deal with the source of their destructive entitlement, in this case, society at large. To simply say, "This is the way I was raised," continues to breed heterosexual guilt. The constructive entitlement comes from becoming politically active and attempting to change society, or at least the therapist's relationship with society. This can be done on several levels. For example, heterosexual therapists can become involved in political activism such as rallies or letter writing campaigns. Or, they can serve mentoring positions to the GLB community or train other therapists or students to work with GLB clients. They can also be change agents by participating in GLB scholarship. Certainly, part of my work on this issue is writing this paper.

As I continue with the process of dealing with my own homophobia, I am more comfortable in dealing with the homophobic issues of my GLB clients. My ability to face these issues in an intimate manner enables them to also face their internalized homophobia. In some cases, this revitalized intimacy with self facilitates intimate dialogue with their same-sex partners. In turn, these successes foster a greater sense in me to work more on myself, which in turn continues the process with my GLB clients.

CONCLUSION

My role as a therapist with GLB clients is a work in progress. It is a journey marked by mistakes, self-doubt, guilt, and ultimately many rewards. Besides the positive feeling of having helped some truly wonderful people along the way, I have also faced many of my own issues and have grown as a person. This has been a scary, embarrassing, and painful paper to write. In the process, I have had to look at myself with a critical eye that I have not found particularly pleasant. Then again, I also feel a sense of pride and personal growth from what I have done. Do I need more work on my issues? The answer is a definitive, "Yes!" But then, much more work needs to be done by all of us.

REFERENCES

Anderson, H. (1997). *Conversation, language, and possibilities: A postmodern approach to therapy.* New York: Basic Books.

Bernstein, A.C. (2000). Straight therapists working with lesbians and gays in family therapy. *Journal of Marital & Family Therapy, 26,* 443-454.

Boszormenyi-Nagy, I. & Krasner, B.R. (1986). *Between give & take: A clinical guide to contextual therapy.* New York: Bunner/Mazel.

Green, R.J. (2003). When therapists do not want their clients to be homosexual: A response to Rosik's article. *Journal of Marital & Family Therapy, 29,* 29-38.

Long, J.K. (1996). Working with lesbians, gays, and bisexuals: Addressing heterosexism in supervision. *Family Process, 35,* 377-388.

Stone-Fish, L., & Coole, D.A. (2002). Difficult dialogues: Coming out in family therapy. American Association for Marriage and Family Therapy 60th Annual Conference. Cincinnati, OH.

Thomas, V., Karis, T.A., & Wetchler, J.L. (2003). Clinical issues with interracial couples. Binghamton, NY: The Haworth Press, Inc.

White, M. (1995). *Re-authoring lives: Interviews & essays.* Adelaide, South Australia: Dulwich Centre Publications.

Resources on Same-Sex Couples for Therapists and Clients

Debra Wallace

Kevin P. Lyness

SUMMARY. This article provides a brief annotated bibliography of re-sources for working with same-sex couples. We provide summaries of articles, book chapters, books, and web sites which we have found to be particularly helpful in working with same sex couples. Books covered include those targeted to therapists as well as those targeted to clients (self-help and bibliotherapy books). *[Article copies available for a fee from The Haworth Document Delivery Service: 1-800-HAWORTH. E-mail address: <docdelivery@haworthpress.com> Website: <http://www.HaworthPress.com> © 2004 by The Haworth Press, Inc. All rights reserved.]*

KEYWORDS. Same sex couples, annotated bibliography, resources

Gays and lesbians seek therapy for many of the same reasons that hetero-sexual individuals do (i.e., depression, anxiety, substance abuse). However, they may be less likely to come for issues regarding their sexual identity (i.e.,

Debra Wallace, BS, is a Master's Degree student in the Marriage and Family Therapy Program, Colorado State University, Fort Collins, CO.

Kevin P. Lyness, PhD, is Assistant Professor, Human Development and Family Studies, Colorado State University, Fort Collins, CO 80523-1570.

[Haworth co-indexing entry note]: "Resources on Same-Sex Couples for Therapists and Clients." Wallace, Debra, and Kevin P. Lyness. Co-published simultaneously in *Journal of Couple & Relationship Therapy* (The Haworth Press) Vol. 3, No. 2/3, 2004, pp. 147-155; and: *Relationship Therapy with Same-Sex Couples* (ed: Jerry J. Bigner, and Joseph L. Wetchler) The Haworth Press, Inc., 2004, pp. 147-155. Single or multiple copies of this article are available for a fee from The Haworth Document Delivery Service [1-800-HAWORTH, 9:00 a.m. - 5:00 p.m. (EST). E-mail address: docdelivery@haworthpress.com].

http://www.haworthpress.com/web/JCRT

Digital Object Identifier: 10.1300/J398v03n02_14

couple problems) due to concerns about homophobia. Also, values, norms, and coping strategies needed to live as a sexual minority in a heterosexual culture are often unclear. Same-sex couples may not even consider couple therapy as a viable resource. It is up to helping professionals to create more opportunities to assist same-sex couples.

Therapists have a responsibility to educate themselves about same-sex couples and the issues that are faced by these couples. Therapists should be knowledgeable about the diversity within same-sex relationships as well as common issues. They should be able to expel myths about same-sex relationships. Most importantly, they should explore their own biases about same-sex couples to prevent counter-transference feelings from hindering the therapeutic relationship and positive outcomes.

Many therapists also utilize *bibliotherapy*. Bibliotherapy is a legitimate strategy that enables individuals to empower themselves and better their relationships. It has been reviewed for effectiveness and found to be as effective as therapist-administered treatments (Marrs, 1995). There are several books that may be appropriate bibliotherapy assignments for same-sex couples which therapists should be aware of.

Below, we review a sample articles, book chapters, books, and websites that have relevance for therapists treating same-sex couples.

ARTICLES

Chesley, L. C., MacAulay, D., & Ristock, J. L. (1998). *Abuse in lesbian relationships: Information and resources.* Retrieved on December 29, 2002, from: *http://www.hc-sc.gc.ca/hppb/familyviolence/pdfs/lesbianabuse.pdf*

The authors are counselors and wrote this report based on their experience of working with lesbians reporting violence in their relationships. They provide guidelines for lesbians, friends, and helping professionals responding to lesbian abuse. They address the diversity within the lesbian experience and the social context surrounding lesbianism.

Eldridge, N. S. (1987). Gender issues in counseling same-sex couples. *Professional Psychology: Research and Practice, 18,* 567-572.

This article addresses barriers that can hinder therapist's ability to work with gay and lesbian clients. The author explores how the therapist's own stereotypes, heterosexual bias, and tendency to overemphasize gender in intimate relationships influence counseling. The author suggests guidelines for therapist and educators working with gay and lesbian clients.

Keller, D., & Rosen, H. (1988). Treating the gay couple within the context of their families of origin. [Report] *Family Therapy Collections. 25,* 105-119.

This article stresses the importance of a healthy, loving, and growing intimate relationship between gay men. It takes a comprehensive family therapy approach to exploring the issues that impede the development of gay men's relationships. It provides a model for assessing family-of-origin issues that are affecting each partner in the relationship.

Lehman, M. (1997). *At the end of the rainbow: A report on gay male domestic violence and abuse.* Retrieved on December 29, 2002, from: *http://www.gaypartnerabuseproject.org/text/research.doc* .

The author explores "the patterns, forms, frequency and impact of domestic violence and abuse on battered gay and bisexual men as well as their help-seeking behaviors and reasons for remaining in abusive relationships" (p. 4). He defines various types of abuse, provides a literature review of domestic violence, integrates sociological, psychological, and multidimensional perspective theories, and confronts myths.

Meyer, J. (1989). Guess who's coming to dinner this time? A study of gay intimate relationships and the support for those relationships. *Marriage & Family Review, 14* (3-4), 59-82.

This paper compares long-term gay and heterosexual intimate relationships. It explores the support systems that each of these relationships receive within their communities. The goal of the paper is to increase readers' understanding of the success and failures of gay couples. A section discusses the impact of AIDS on intimate gay relationships. It suggests areas of study for further investigation regarding support for the gay community.

Miller, A. J., Bobner, R. F., & Zarski, J. J. (2000). Sexual identity development: A base for work with same-sex couple partner abuse. *Contemporary Family Therapy, 22,* 189-200.

This article highlights the differences between same-sex battering and heterosexual battering. It makes suggestions regarding the interaction between domestic violence and sexual identity development stages of same-sex partners. It reviews treatment recommendations unique to treating same-sex couples involved in violent relationships.

BOOK CHAPTERS

Goldenberg, H. & Goldenberg, I. (1998). Counseling gay males and lesbian couples. In *Counseling today's families* (pp. 223-254). Pacific Grove, CA: Brooks/Cole.

This chapter serves as a brief introduction for therapists counseling same-sex couples. It highlights the differences between same-sex and opposite-sex partners, common myths about same-sex couples, and possible problems that occur in same-sex relationships. It provides some counseling guidelines and information about HIV and AIDS counseling.

Patterson, D. G., Ciabattari, T., & Schwartz, P. (1999). The constraints of innovation: Commitment and stability among same-sex couples. In J. M. Adams & W. H. Jones (Eds.), *Handbook of interpersonal commitment and relationship stability: Perspectives on individual differences* (pp. 339-359). New York: Kluwer Academic/Plenum.

The function of this chapter is to explore how gay and lesbian couples manage to create secure commitments. The authors also compare perceptions about gay and lesbian relationships. The chapter highlights the external and internal influences that are unique to noninstitutionalized relationships that shape same-sex couple's commitment.

Rutter, V., & Schwartz, P. (2000). Gender, marriage, and diverse possibilities for cross-sex and same-sex pairs. In D. H. Demo, K. R. Allen, & M. Fine (Eds.), *Handbook of family diversity* (pp. 59-81). New York: Oxford University.

This chapter explores the topics of gender and marriage in heterosexual and same-sex couples in committed relationships. The focus is on social structural contexts, sexual expression, and domestic violence. It highlights similarities and differences that exist between cross-sex and same-sex pairs.

Young, M., & Long, L. (1998). Same-sex couples. In *Counseling and therapy for couples* (pp. 300-316). Pacific Grove, CA: Brooks/Cole.

The authors of this chapter address the different issues and stressors same-sex couples face. They address special difficulties that same-sex couples have with families, work situations, and the legal system. They explore the lack of role models for same-sex couples and the problems that arise when same-sex couples try to fit into traditional marriage models. Scenarios for role-plays and discussions are provided.

BOOKS

Alexander, C. (Ed.). (1996). *Gay and lesbian mental health: A sourcebook for practitioners*. New York: Harrington Park.

This book challenges stereotypes about homosexuality and provides information about recent changes and findings regarding gay and lesbian mental health. The book serves to broaden reader's perspective and comprehension regarding the lives of gays and lesbians. The authors of the chapters are clinicians or educators who have experience with the topic area they write about. The topics that pertain to couple issues are balancing autonomy and intimacy in relationships, parenting, and working with partners of sexual abuse survivors. Other chapters address suicide, grief and loss, vulnerability to body dissatisfaction and eating disorders, identity development of gay Latinos, and aging. Integrating religious and spiritual needs in psychotherapy and working with parents of gay and lesbian children is also covered. This book is ideal for therapists.

Berzon, B. (1990). *Permanent partners: Building gay and lesbian relationships that last*. New York: Dutton.

A psychotherapist who specializes in working with gay and lesbian couples wrote this book for therapists and their clients. She provides advice on internal and external problems that occur when gay or lesbian couples choose to build a life together. The purpose of the book is to enable couples to gain perspective on their relationship, to identify stressors that may be inhibiting the growth of their partnership, and develop new strategies for dealing with stressors. The chapters explore relationship myths, power and control issues, jealousy, sexual desire differences, in-laws, and children.

Berzon, B. (1996). *The intimacy dance: A guide to long-term success in gay and lesbian relationships*. New York: Penguin.

The author draws on her own experiences from her professional practice and her long-term partnership to help couples improve communication and normalize transitions. This book walks the reader through the stages of gay and lesbian relationships and common issues that may arise. She addresses the concerns of merging identities, waning sex, resolving conflicts, competing career demands, illnesses, and mid-life crises. This book includes a chapter about the benefits of couples counseling. This author's books are meant to reach a diverse group of gays and lesbians so not all the material will relate to each couple. This book is ideal for clients.

Carl, D. (1990). *Counseling same-sex couples*. New York: Norton.

The author of this book gives readers a multilevel description of same-sex couple's issues, supports, and difficulties over the life span. He applies basic family therapy theory and systemic orientation to meet the needs of same-sex couples. The author has 15 years of clinical experience and has a supervisor and teaching background. He offers personal observations of gays and lesbians and their families, and brings to light their opinions and insights. The book focuses more on gay male relationships than lesbian relationships, but offers some distinctions between the two relationships. Pre-coupling and coupling considerations are explored. Specific issues pertaining to parenting, blended families, AIDS, and alcohol and drug use are addressed. The author examines theoretical and practical concerns regarding couples counseling and provides some interventions. This book aims to make therapists more effective when working with same-sex couples and is a must read for all therapists.

Cabaj, R. P., & Purcell, D. W. (Eds.). (1998). *On the road to same-sex marriage: A supportive guide to psychological, political, and legal issues.* San Francisco: Jossey-Bass.

This book discusses the history and development of gay and lesbian marriage while addressing psychological and legal issues. Various chapters explore how and why same-sex relationships are formed, how they differ from heterosexual relationships, and the impressions legally sanctioned same-sex marriages may have on emotional, psychological, legal, and child rearing issues. Most of the book focuses on civil marriages, yet one chapter does look at religious and spiritual issues regarding same-sex marriage. International trends in same-sex marriages are also examined. The authors hope this book will serve as a tool in the fight for gay and lesbian civil, legal, and human rights. The Appendix contains a resource list of books pertaining to same-sex marriages. This book is helpful for both therapists and clients.

Clunis, D., & Green, G. (1988). *Lesbian couples.* Seattle: Seal.

Two experienced lesbian therapists wrote this book for lesbian couples. Their purpose is to guide lesbians through the pleasures and challenges of being part of a couple. Although some topics covered are common to all couples, some are specific to lesbian couples like coming out to family and friends, monogamy and non-monogamy, and separateness and togetherness. This book also incorporates issues concerning differences in race, class, age, and physical ability, as well as addresses the problems caused by substance abuse or history of sexual abuse. This book is particularly helpful for clients.

Dworkin, S. H., & Gutierrez, F. J. (Eds.). (1992). *Counseling gay men and lesbians: Journey to the end of the rainbow.* Alexandria, VA: American Association for Counseling and Development (now the American Counseling Association).

This book demonstrates effective techniques utilized by gay-, lesbian-, and bisexual-affirmative practitioners. It addresses the practical aspects of working with gay, lesbian, and bisexual clients. The chapters are organized under five sections: developmental issues, marriage and family counseling, diverse populations, incidents of violence, and counseling techniques. Some of the topics covered include career counseling for gays and lesbians, counseling older gay men, counseling lesbian couples, incest survivors, survivors of anti-gay violence, and raising children. There are chapters dedicated to Asian Americans and Latin populations. There is also a chapter about the biases of psychological tests. A list of professional associations and resources is included. This book is good for therapists.

Evosevich, J.M., & Avriette, M. (2000). *The gay and lesbian psychotherapy treatment planner*. New York: Wiley.

The purpose of this book is to help professionals working with gays and lesbians to develop focused, formal treatment plans that satisfy all of the demands of HMOs, managed care companies, third-party payers, and state and federal review agencies. The authors write from the perspective that appropriate treatment of gays and lesbians requires acceptance of sexual orientation. The book is organized around 27 main presenting problems. The chapters that are specifically related to couples include: adoption/surrogacy, female and male sexual dysfunction, HIV negative/HIV positive couples, intimate relationship conflicts, parenting conflicts and separation. The book describes the behavioral manifestations of each problem, the long-term goals and short-term objectives of treatment, and clinically tested treatment options. This book is ideal for therapists.

Greenan, D. E., & Tunnell, G. (2003). *Couple therapy with gay men*. New York: Guilford.

This book serves as a basic introduction to therapists who are interested in learning about the interpersonal dynamics that all men share as well as characteristics that are specific to gay couples. The authors provide a three-stage clinical model based on structural family therapy to guide therapist's interventions. Heterosexism, gender acculturation, homophobia, and gay identity formation are explored within the contexts of therapy sessions and the gay couple relationship. This book is particularly helpful for therapists.

Laird, J., & Green, R. (Eds.). (1996). *Lesbians and gays in couples and families: A handbook for therapists*. San Francisco: Jossey-Bass.

This book comprehensively explores what couple and family relationships of lesbians and gays are like, including myths and misconceptions. It is meant to guide therapist's learning processes regarding their own biases, as well as family theory and practice. It pays special attention to social and political influences as well as the unique diversity within the gay and lesbian population. It is broken down into four sections: personal, professional, and political contexts; families of origin; lesbian and gay couples; and lesbian and gay parents. There is a chapter where a straight therapist and gay therapist discuss bicultural issues. Chapters specific to couples explore the influence of gender and ethnicity, boundaries, childhood trauma, and chemical dependency. This book is good for therapists.

Marcus, E. (1998). *Together forever: Gay and lesbian marriage*. New York: Anchor.

This is a good book for clients. The author takes the readers through the lives of 40 gay and lesbian couples in happy, long-lasting relationships. The couples have been together from nine to fifty years, ranged in age from 31 to

86, and came from diverse backgrounds. A variety of issues are discussed like, roles and gender, money, work, sex, family, aging, and loss. The author asks all the couples "What is a happy relationship?" and "Is there a secret to a happy relationship?" and relays his findings to the readers. Some examples of "secrets" are patience, honesty, and acceptance. By reading this book, couples can learn about what works in long-term, same-sex relationships. This book provides positive role models for same-sex couples as well as normalizes their experiences.

Ritter, K. Y., & Terndrup, A. I. (2002). *Handbook of affirmative psychotherapy with lesbians and gay men.* New York: Guilford.

This book is a comprehensive resource for therapists wanting affirmative techniques and interventions for their gay, lesbian, and bisexual clients. The authors both have extensive experience as advocates and clinicians. They address assessment and treatment concerns such as psychodiagnostic errors and working with culturally diverse clients. The book delves into sociocultural factors influencing gay and lesbian mental health, identity formation, and developmental tasks and transitions. Certain chapters address couple concerns regarding working with same-sex couples and their families, and sexual issues. A resource section of publications, advocacy groups, and Web-based resources is included. This book is a great tool for therapists.

Wingspan Domestic Violence Project. (2000). *Domestic violence in the gay, lesbian, bisexual, transgender community: A resource 2000.* [Booklet]. Tucson, AZ: Author.

This publication goes in depth into domestic violence (DV) in gay, lesbian, bisexual and transgender (GLBT) relationships. It helps readers to try to understand this complex problem through the use of the power and control wheel, the equity wheel, and the cycle of violence chart. It addresses specific concerns regarding the GLBT community, dispels myths about GLBT domestic violence, and provides interventions. It describes the legal response to DV in GLBT communities as well as the process of working with batterers. A list of related publications and videos is provided. This booklet is good for both therapists and clients.

WEB SITES

http://www.advocate.com/

This is an award-winning national gay and lesbian newspaper available online. The newspaper has news, health, entertainment, and events sections as well as special columns and polls. The site provides access to the *Advocate's* archives, recent issue, and links to other great resources.

http://www.buddybuddy.com/

This website was created by Partners Task Force for Gay and Lesbian Couples. It is a national resource for same-sex couples. It is constantly updated and contains a plethora of essays, legal articles, surveys, and resources about legal marriage, relationships, parenting, and immigration.

http://www.gayparentmag.com/29181.html

This website is a list of support groups around the country for GLBT parents. The site is maintained by *Gay Parent* magazine which is published bi-monthly and distributed across the U.S. The magazine's focus is to support and empower GLBT parents. You can access back issues and other resources through this site.

http://www.gaypartnerabuseproject.org/

This website is maintained by a Canadian community based, non-profit organization. They provide support, education and advocacy for men who experience violence and abuse in intimate same-sex relationships.

http://www.gaypasg.org/

This website is maintained by Gay and Lesbian Political Action and Support Groups. The site includes up to date gay and lesbian headlines from the national press. It lists current projects that are underway. Other resourceful links are also provided.

http://www.glnh.org/

The Gay and Lesbian National Hotline (GLNH) is a non-profit organization which provides nationwide toll-free peer-counseling, information and referrals. Their website includes their phone number and e-mail address to contact them directly with any questions. The site has links to local resources and other national organizations.

http://www.hrc.org/

This website is sponsored by the Human Rights Campaign and provides access to many GLBT resources. It has a search engine that locates employees providing domestic partner benefits.

http://www.lgbtcenters.org/

This site is produced by the National Association of Lesbian, Gay, Bisexual, and Transgender Community Centers. The site provides a search that lists over 100 nationwide GLBT centers.

http://www.mftsource.com/Treatment.gaylesbian.htm

This website is put out by MFTSource and is designed to assist marriage and family therapists seeking resources for treating gays, lesbians, and bisexuals. Users may select a resource with links to more information.

Index

Numbers followed by "f" indicate figures; "t" following a page number indicates tabular material.